THIRTY DAYS IN QUITO
Two Gringos and a Three-Legged Cat Move to Ecuador

K. Kris Loomis

Get a FREE short story at www.kkrisloomis.com!

Published by Lililoom Publishing
Copyright © 2017 K. Kris Loomis
ISBN: 9781520902586

Dedication

For Hugh and Triplet, my adventure buddies.

Author's Note

I would like to thank my beta readers, Michelle Cornish, Mary Houkal, Shoon Ledyard, and Linda Price for their time and interest in my project. They provided valuable feedback and I am grateful for their insights.

Also, a heartfelt thank you to my awesome editor, Ann Wilson.

And, finally, a big thank you to my first reader and travel companion through life, Hugh Loomis.

ALSO BY K. KRIS LOOMIS

How to Sneak More Yoga Into Your Life: A Doable Yoga Plan for Busy People

How to Sneak More Meditation Into Your Life: A Doable Meditation Plan for Busy People

The Monster In the Closet and Other Stories

Learn more about K. Kris Loomis and get a FREE short story at www.kkrisloomis.com!

Forward

My South American adventure began the summer after I turned forty-five. Up until that point in my life, I had only lived in the state of South Carolina.

I love South Carolina for many reasons. No matter where I am in the state, I can travel to the mountains or the coast for a quickie vacation in a matter of hours (road trips!). My entire family, both immediate and distant, lives in the state (yeah, I know, not always a bonus, but family is family, right?). I love the fact that the state has four distinct, beautiful seasons, and although some years the summers can be brutal, I have never in my life had to shovel snow (a definite bonus!).

Even though I am not the most traveled person in the world, I am one of those annoying people who cannot sit still. I am in perpetual learning mode, taking on subjects such as chess, origami, crochet, backgammon, mnemonics, sudoku, and yoga, all after age thirty. My longest 'learning' love affair has been with the piano. My father began teaching me the instrument when I was six years old, and to this day I never tire of practicing or teaching others how to play.

I have not had a perfect life, but I've had a really good life. And even though I've had some rough patches (don't we all), the love and support of my family and steadfast friends has made my life rich, interesting, and pretty darn enjoyable.

So why would I leave all this wonderfulness to move to South America?

In May of 2009, I married a free spirit named Hugh. He had always dreamed of retiring somewhere in Central or South America and had even taken several trips to Costa Rica through the years to check it out. He was working in the mortgage business when all hell broke loose in 2007 and he ended up retiring a few years later, way ahead of schedule.

We had a shared office in our home at that time, and occasionally he would send me a link about a cool place to retire. I would open his email, hurriedly skim the contents, then promptly send it to the trash. I mean, come on. I was teaching piano full time and had over forty students. Besides, I was too young to think about this retirement nonsense.

One day he sent a link that listed the top ten retirement destinations for American retirees the previous year. Ecuador was number one on the list and had been in the top three for the past ten years. Now I never seriously considered picking up and moving somewhere, especially another country, because I had a good job! I had family obligations! I only spoke English! We couldn't afford it! I mean, come on, I couldn't stop working in my mid-forties.

Who does that?

But something that day made me stop and think. How would I feel if Hugh made it to the end of his life and had never had the opportunity to realize his dream of living abroad? Would it kill me to take a chance? After all, think of all the new things I could learn in a different country! And, if I've learned one thing about life it's that nothing is ever permanent. We could have an adventure for a year or two, and if we decided it wasn't for us we could always return to the states, right?

After exhaustive research, we decided to fly to Ecuador to see if we could picture ourselves living there and to find out if we really could afford to live solely off Hugh's social security like the magazines said we could. We signed up for a whirlwind ten-day tour in Ecuador that covered the Northern Sierras (Quito and Otavalo), the coast (Manta, Puerto Lopez, Canoa, and Guayaquil), and part of the Southern Sierras (Cuenca).

We arrived back in the United States exhausted, but of one mind. The following spring we sold our house and all our belongings to raise enough money to move to South America.

I had been invigorated by new learning possibilities in the past, and, considering everyone in my family lives a long time I figured I had practically an entire second lifetime waiting to be defined. So, I thought, why not? If we didn't have an adventure now, when would we? It may sound cliché, but I have always believed that life is precious, and when it's gone, it's not just gone, it is forever gone.

We moved to South America in July of 2013.

Our first stop: Quito, Ecuador.

Prologue Part One: Is That Cat Wearing a Shirt?

I left my Mother crying at the airport. I knew my Father wouldn't be able to console her, because even though he wasn't sobbing like she was, I knew he was conflicted and sad to see his only daughter, who had never lived more than a couple hours away, fly off into the unknown.

Hugh and I weren't even sure we would be able to leave that day because one of Ecuador's active volcanoes, Volcán Tungurahua, blew its top the day before and if the wind blew the ash a certain direction the Quito International Airport would have to close for who knew how long.

This is a scenario we hadn't anticipated. Sure, we knew Ecuador had volcanos, but knowing that fact did not prepare us for the 'Throat of Fire' wreaking havoc on our international moving plans.

We constantly checked our online resources that morning and were finally satisfied that the wind would continue to blow in our favor. So after lunch, we loaded our four fifty pound suitcases, thirty pounds of carry-on, and Triplet (the cat) into my mother's SUV and rode in virtual silence as my parents drove us to the Charlotte-Douglas International Airport in North Carolina.

We unloaded our suitcases and the cat as quickly as we could outside the terminal. I didn't think I would be able to make it through a long goodbye, so I gave a quick hug to my parents and darted inside the airport before I could think too much about leaving everything I had ever known behind.

We only had two hours to pay the extra fee for taking a cat with us and pass international security before our 3:30 Delta flight took off. The line to pay for the cat was long, but, thankfully, moved quickly. We lugged our load into the security line and dug out all our liquids and paperwork like good little passengers.

Now, I had never flown with a pet before, so I didn't know what to expect. I guess I thought I would just carry her in her little travel carrier through the detector with me. Come to find out, I was only half right.

Her pet carrier had to go through on the conveyer belt, but SHE had to go through with me. In my arms. Which meant I had to take her out of the carrier. With hundreds of noisy and unhappy people surrounding us and all sorts of bells, whistles, and walkie talkies going off. AND the agent insisted on swabbing my hands for explosive residue. WHILE HOLDING THE CAT. I have scars on my shoulder to commemorate that part of the journey.

Once everyone was satisfied that neither the cat nor I was planning on blowing up the plane that afternoon, I was allowed to return her to her carrier. As I was stuffing her back in, a young agent with tightly woven dreads looked at me and said, "Is that cat wearing a shirt?"

The cat was, indeed, wearing a shirt. A 'thunder shirt.' The snug fitting little vest for cats and dogs that supposedly reduces anxiety from thunder, vet visits, curious children, and various animal psychoses. I wanted to do everything I could to ensure a smooth flight for all involved, so after opting not to drug her for the flight I coughed up the cash for this tiny little shirt to hug my cat for me all the way to Ecuador.

A Short Interlude: Why We Decided Not to Drug Our Cat

Any cat owner will tell you that one of the worst things about having cats is that, eventually, you have to take them to the vet. Cats DO NOT like being stuffed in little carriers (most cat lovers bear lasting reminders of that fact) and they make their displeasure loud and clear by mewing at the top of their little kitty lungs drowning out the radio in the car all the way to the vet's office.

When we decided to move to Ecuador with our cat, Triplet, I began worrying about the logistics of her being in that confined space for so long and how much she might annoy our neighbors on the plane. Would she totally freak out? Would she cry the entire way? Nobody likes a fussy baby on a plane, so I was pretty sure nobody would appreciate a fussy cat, either.

So, on Triplet's last doctor visit before we left, my husband and I asked the vet if there were any options for calming her on the trip. Airline policy clearly states that an animal has to be awake before it will be allowed to fly, so we knew we couldn't just knock her out. Our vet suggested a tiny dose of valium, just to take the edge off. I told her I thought that was a grand idea, but what were we going to do with Triplet?

She gave us a couple of pills for Triplet (none for me, darn it!) and said we might want to do a trial run before we left so we would know how she might react. Hugh and I thought that was a good idea, so we took her home, stuffed a pill down her throat (not an easy or fun task), then left to run a few errands.

We were expecting to find a groovy chilled-out kitty on our return, but what we found was a falling down drunk and terrified cat. Maybe now is a good time to mention that Triplet has only three legs.

Triplet had wandered into our yard and our lives a year and a half earlier. She was a pitiful creature at that time with her black coat hanging loosely on her small frame and her little eyes all droopy and sad. She was so tiny we thought she was a kitten, except she had a disproportionally large head. The vet said she was probably at least four years old and was only that small because she was starving. She had been spayed and her leg had been surgically removed, so at one time she had been cared for, but something had obviously gone very wrong for her along the way.

We don't know how she ended up in our yard, or how long she had been trying to survive out on her own with only three legs. We tried to find her owner by putting out flyers and calling the local vets, but no one was looking for a three-legged black cat. That's when she became part of our family.

We have no idea what happened to her leg. I've asked her several times, but she's not ready to talk about it yet.

What we found when we returned from running our errands that day was heartbreaking. Triplet had lost all equilibrium which was magnified by her not having that back leg. She had fallen and knocked her food bowl over, so kibble was everywhere, and she had managed to turn her water bowl over, so water was everywhere. She was soaking wet on one side and her eyes were wide with panic. Her little heart was racing and she couldn't stand up without immediately falling back down. I ended up having to hold her like a baby for the next five hours until the drugs finally wore off so she wouldn't hurt herself.

That's why we decided not to drug our cat for the journey, and why she arrived at the airport wearing a shirt.

Prologue Part Two: Is That Cat Wearing a Shirt?

"Is that cat wearing a shirt?" the agent with tightly woven dreads asked.

I told the young lady that, yes, the cat was wearing a shirt. She wrinkled her nose and said, "Well, I ain't never seen that before." Truth be told, neither had I. I was beginning to wonder if they made 'thunder shirts' for humans.

We flew to Atlanta first because it cost $150.00 LESS each ticket to fly from Charlotte to Atlanta first rather than take a direct flight from Charlotte to Quito. Don't 'cha love airline logic? Then, after a two movie flight from Atlanta to Quito, we arrived safe and sound in Ecuador at 10:15 that evening.

Triplet was not amused when I had to take her out of her traveling cocoon at the customs counter in Quito, but at least we didn't have to go through the explosives song and dance again. After we collected our bags, we waded through a sea of Spanish and finally spotted Hugh's name on a waving placard.

A cheery, middle-aged Ecuadorian woman led us to a waiting taxi where we overrode all laws of physics and somehow managed to get all four suitcases, our carry-on bags, the cat, and ourselves into what was, I swear, a clown-car. That vehicle was made for Lilliputians, not robust American men like my husband. But Hugh was a good sport and, although our non-English-speaking cabbie drove as if he were on the final lap of the Indie 500, he did get us to our hostel safe and sound.

After we checked in and stored our suitcases behind the desk, the owner of the place, Dom, said he would show us up to our room. As we stepped outside to make our way to the stairs a distinct odor engulfed us. Dom said, "Do you smell that?" I replied, "Yes. I do." He said, "I think someone is smoking pot." I said, "Yes. It would appear so."

Welcome to Ecuador.

Days One ~ Ten

Day One Part One: About That Shower

We didn't think we would be able to sleep that first night in the hostel, but after downing a bottle of wine, setting up Triplet's litter box and making sure she had food and fresh water, about all we had to do was slip off our shoes and we were out.

We were awakened the next morning by the sun peeking through the paper thin yellow curtains around 6:15. Wow, I thought. I just woke up in Ecuador. Wow.

At breakfast that morning, we were able see more of the hostel in the daylight. This was a new place, small but cozy, clean, and designed with lots of natural light in mind. Many businesses had sprung up around the rechristened Quito airport (ironically, now over an hour away from Quito) since it opened earlier that year.

The previous year when we toured the country, we stayed in some nice hostels, but most of them had a little age on them. Not exactly run down, let's just say well stayed in. Here, in Dom's hostel, mostly because of the modernity factor, I had high hopes for an exceptional shower that morning.

You see, on our scouting trip I never once had a good shower...not ONE decent shower in ten days. Not one! Most showers in Ecuador are heated by gas, which is subsidized by the government and very inexpensive. Everything is wonderful until you get to the bottom of the tank, and then, just like that, you are left shivering and spitting out a few choice words. How could it be that, out of our entire tour group I was always the lucky one that ended up meeting the bottom of the tank? Every. Single. Time.

Now I am not a shower hog, but I have been accustomed to having hot water for at least ten minutes at a time pretty much my entire life. Summer camp? Hot water. College dorm? Hot water. France? Mexico? Glorious hot water. Even on long camping trips, I was able to pull off a decent shower somewhere along the way.

So, that first morning in our newly adopted country I was expecting to hit the reset button and have a fresh shower start. The initial signs were promising. Good water pressure, steam opening my sinuses, non-slip surface in the shower stall. So far, so good. Then, right after I lathered my face, BAM! No hot water. I had to settle for a half-shower, and poor Hugh settled for no shower.

Not a great way to start our new life in Ecuador, but, hey. It could only go up from there, right?

Day One Part Two: The Penthouse

Shower aside, we were still psyched that morning because we were going to be reunited with Sarah, the owner of the tour company we used on our scouting trip. Sarah is an American who went to Ecuador as a Peace Corps volunteer in the 1990's and fell in love, not only with the country, but also with a man (probably not in that order). She married an Ecuadorian general and decided to stay in the country to raise her family. She is knowledgeable, capable, sensitive to Ecuadorian culture, always ready to jump in and help, and a lot of fun to be around. I wished I could fold her up and carry her around in my pocket.

We contacted her soon after we made our decision to move and asked her to help us find an apartment in Quito. Our plan was to start there so we could secure our residency visas, then we would decide where in the country we wanted to settle more permanently.

Sarah arrived at the hostel to pick us up at 10:00 that morning. I was anxious to get going because Triplet did not seem to be adjusting well to the hostel room. The noises in the hall were freaking her out, so much so that she didn't eat, drink, pee, or poo the entire evening or morning we were there, and this after a full day of flying the friendly skies with no litter box in sight.

The plan was for Sarah to pick us up and take us into North Quito to look at an apartment I had seen on the internet, exactly one block from the old Quito airport location. We were looking forward to seeing this one bedroom, fully furnished apartment near the emerging Bicentennial Park (the city of Quito was in the process of turning the abandoned airstrips into a park) because, since having sold our house several weeks prior, we had been vagabonds. While it was wonderful spending time here and there with our loved ones before we left I was ready to be still and in one place for awhile.

So, after saying farewell to the crappy shower at the hostel late that morning, we arrived at the apartment, which, it turned out, was part of a house. Houses in Ecuador, especially in the cities, are not freestanding on separate lots like they are in the states. They are connected, like what we see with townhouses.

After looking in vain for a bell or buzzer, we banged on the iron gate out front for about ten minutes with Sarah's car keys. This 'key-banging' episode is quite common in Ecuador and would repeat itself on many occasions during our adventures.

Eventually, a young man appeared and said he could show us the apartment. So we left the suitcases in the car, grabbed the cat, and followed Patricio, the landlady's son, into the building. That's when we discovered the 'fully furnished one bedroom' apartment we were so excited about was, in reality, a 4th floor walk up studio apartment on top of the roof with two bean bag chairs, a naked mattress, and a small table. No stove. No refrigerator. No pots, pans, sheets, dishes, towels. Nada! We quickly deflated.

Sarah told Patricio that we had been led to believe this was a furnished apartment. He asked what we needed. We told him a good start would be sheets.

He disappeared, then returned with his lovely wife Sofia, his young daughter Camila, and a set of, if not clean, at least *almost* clean sheets. They asked what else we needed, so, with Sarah's help, we were able to communicate a few other basics we felt would get us through the weekend until we could find more appropriate accommodations. We didn't have any other options, except to try and find a hostel that would accept a cat, and Sarah said most hostels didn't accept pets.

Patricio said "OK!" and disappeared again.

So, again with Sarah's help, we hauled the four fifty pound suitcases, three carry-on bags, and the cat's provisions up the four flights of stairs. Not easy, given that Quito is over 9000 feet above sea level. I like to think that I am in pretty good shape, but after all that huffin' and puffin' up the four flights to the roof several times I thought either I was going to become a widow or my husband was going to become a widower that day. I've never sucked wind like that before in my life. Oh, and if the altitude didn't kill us I was sure we would be done in by the stairs. Think Alfred Hitchcock's *The Spiral Staircase* with NO HANDRAIL!

We saw no sign of Patricio, so Sarah suggested we take a quick trip to the nearest grocery store, the SuperMaxi. Our friend in the states, Howard, later said it sounded like a feminine hygiene product to him (I didn't want to tell him that the SuperMaxi is a sister store to the MegaMaxi, you know, for those heavy days). So off we went to get a few provisions at the nearest SuperMaxi. Considering we had no way to cook, we didn't get much that first day: some bottled water (yeah, it's true you shouldn't drink the water most places in Ecuador), some peanut butter, a sleeve of Ritz crackers, a broom, toilet paper, and a couple of trash cans. I told Hugh I felt like I was in college again.

By the time we got back to the penthouse (lemonade, folks, making lemonade here) the landlady, Nora, was home. She, of course, wanted the rent. After we begrudgingly handed over the money, she disappeared. And after holding our hands all day Sarah had to get back to her family.

So we were left alone in an empty 'penthouse' on a flat roof in the middle of a foreign country. The fact that we were exhausted, frustrated, and the cat had still not peed or pooed led us to the unanimous decision to end the day as quickly as possible and hope that *something* positive would happen the next day to squash our disappointment and rekindle our excitement. We turned off the lights and crawled in bed at the ungodly hour of 8:00.

We had just dozed off when we heard BAM BAM BAM on the apartment door. We stumbled out of bed and found Patricio and Sofia on the other side of the door with a brand new stove and refrigerator (think college dorm size here, but, you know, a fridge is a fridge), as well as pots, pans, plates, glasses, towels, tablecloth, sofa, dish drain, and a bookshelf. It felt like Christmas!

After Patricio set up our gas stove, we fell back in bed feeling much better about our upcoming stay in Quito. Now, if Triplet would just get reacquainted with the litter box...

Day Two: The Box

We woke up that second day (still in Ecuador...wow) and found the frustrations of the previous day had wondrously been replaced with renewed excitement and optimism. Maybe we had only needed some good shut-eye.

Hugh went down to one of the Panaderías (bakeries) on our block and got fresh bread and a pack of Juan Valdez instant coffee for breakfast. The bread was fresh and warm and yummy, but we are NOT instant coffee people. We practically worship freshly brewed coffee, the darker the roast, the better.

Ecuadorians, however, were in the midst of a love affair with instant. They considered it a luxury, and even though Ecuador has some of the best coffee in the world, the good stuff could be pretty expensive. Coffee makers weren't cheap, either. And since we didn't have a coffee maker we sucked it up, held our noses, and pretended that the instant was fabulous, dahling! Yeah, we're coffee snobs.

By this time, I was pretty concerned because the cat had still shown no signs of visiting 'the box.' I had my fingers crossed that maybe she just didn't like the litter I brought with us, a pine sawdust type I had chosen because it weighed significantly less than the clumping clay litter we used back home (it's all about weight when you fly, you know). I told Hugh we needed to make a SuperMaxi run for some clay litter in hopes the cat would, well, you know.

And since we had actual appliances we could buy real food this time! Yay!

This brings me, once again, to the shower. I wanted to take one before we set out on our first solo SuperMaxi run. Unfortunately, our little penthouse has what Sarah likes to call, a 'Frankenstein,' or 'suicide' shower. Some call it a 'widow-maker.' The water in this type of shower is not heated by gas, but by electricity.

In a Frankenstein shower, electric wires come directly out of the wall *in the shower* and are *taped* to other wires that are *out in the open* near the shower-head. The electricity is activated when the water is turned on and heats the water as it passes through the shower-head. Right by your head. Loosely taped live wires. Next to splashing water. Really.

Now, in case you are concerned, please know that there was a breaker box right beside the shower that, presumably, would cut off the electricity in case of a problem. Like electrocution. Sarah couldn't personally name anyone who had died in one of these contraptions, but that didn't necessarily make us feel any better.

On the positive side, I didn't have to worry about running out of gas, so I decided to go for it. Besides, the shower was the only place in the apartment that had hot water. What? Yep, neither the kitchen nor the bathroom sink was equipped with hot water. We would find out this is quite common in Ecuador.

What this meant was that we had to fill a bowl with hot water from the shower and cart it to the kitchen whenever we wanted to wash dishes. This also meant that the only way I could wash my face at night was to either take another scary shower or fill another bowl of hot water from the shower and move it to the bathroom sink. I figured if it was good enough for Cleopatra it was good enough for me. Of course, she had peons to boil and deliver *her* water.

After Hugh and I survived our showers we walked the uphill mile to the SuperMaxi (thankfully, this means that it's all downhill when you are bringing your groceries home) where we picked up a few staples and a small box of clay litter.

As soon as we got back to the apartment, I changed the litter in Triplet's box, and BAM! not two minutes later Triplet visited, to paraphrase my favorite *Get Fuzzy* comic strip, the biodome, both numbers one and two Potty Street, THE BOX man! I'm not sure who was more relieved, me or la gata!

We felt we had been sufficiently productive so far that

day, and since we were still learning to breathe at 9,000 feet, we decided to relax the rest of the afternoon. The next day, we were to meet with Nora, the woman we had hired to help us with our residency visas.

Hugh had spoken to Nora's husband several times on the phone before we left the states, and he assured us his wife was an approved government translator and had contacts in the immigration office. He was absolutely positive we would have our residency visas in a matter of weeks. We hoped so because we had already sent him a good sized deposit for their services.

So we now had two important Noras in our lives, Nora Landlady and Visa Nora. Even though I had emailed Visa Nora as soon as we arrived at the hostel, we still hadn't heard from her. We didn't have local phone service yet, so we couldn't call her. Worrying wouldn't help, so after a simple dinner of rice and veggies (so nice to have a stove!), we once again turned in early. We wanted to be refreshed for mañana, and whatever it might bring along with it.

Day Three Part One: Visa Nora and Sarah Saves the Coffee Day

To our relief, the third day did bring Visa Nora. I received an e-mail very early that morning from her saying that we would get together that day. She didn't say when or where we would get together, mind you, but Hugh and I guessed these things somehow magically worked themselves out south of the equator.

Sure enough, about 10:30, Patricio showed up at our penthouse door proclaiming, "There is someone here to see us!" Of course, he meant there was someone here to see *you*, but we knew what he meant.

Hugh and I peeked over the edge of the building, and down there on the street staring up at us was Visa Nora. She yelled that her phone was not working and that she had been banging on the gate for half an hour. Hugh rushed with Patricio to let her in the building, and I hurriedly straightened up our little table from breakfast.

Visa Nora came in, very confident, business-like, and a

little out of breath from climbing the forty-two steps up to our apartment (welcome to my world, Nora). She was wearing a smart tan pantsuit and her voice was low and throaty with a twinge of gravel, kind of like a Latin version of Marlene Dietrich.

To begin our residency process, the papers we brought with us had to be translated into Spanish and that was Visa Nora's first job. So I dug out the precious paperwork that we had been told we would need to be issued Ecuadorian residency.

We were proud of our papers because we had jumped through hoops of fire with flying poison-tipped arrows zipping past our heads to obtain them. Our birth certificates, marriage licenses, divorce papers, proof of income, background checks, all of which had to be certified and apostilled in the issuing state, then approved and stamped at the Ecuadorian Consulate in Atlanta. We had spent many hours, two trips each to Columbia and Atlanta (not to mention all the fees involved) getting our papers in order. We had dealt with government employees at all levels who had no clue what we needed and STILL got it done. Yes, we were damn proud of our papers.

So what did Visa Nora ask for? Our birth certificates and proof of income. That's all. I said, there must be some mistake, we have all these other papers! And she said, well, they are not asking for those anymore. And that was that.

After Visa Nora left us holding our remaining papers (she promised to be in touch soon, whatever that meant), we quickly changed gears because we were expecting a visit from Sarah. She wanted to check up on us and bring us an extra coffee maker she had (Hallelujah!). We were expecting her around 3:00, but 3:00 came and went with no Sarah. 3:45, no Sarah. 4:15, still no Sarah.

We weren't too concerned because Ecuadorians follow 'manana time.' Technically, if you study Spanish in school, you learn the word manana means 'tomorrow' or 'morning.' However, in real South American life, it means some vague time in the future, maybe tomorrow, perhaps the next day, possibly next week. Manana is one of those flexible words that seems to morph in meaning depending on who is using it and in what context.

By 4:45 we assumed she was not coming. This perplexed us because Sarah was very aware of the differences between 'gringo' time and 'manana' time. She's the one who taught us about it when we were on her tour! I wrote her a short email saying I hoped all was well, and I was sorry if she came earlier and we missed her.

About the time I hit 'send' it occurred to me that I was an idiot. I should have realized from the events earlier in the day that in this land of Fort Knox houses WE needed to be on the lookout for HER! How was she supposed to get past the front gate? We had no bell or buzzer, we still had no phone, and there was no way she could have gotten up the stairs to knock on our door. She could have been down on the street being mauled by a grizzly bear and we wouldn't have known it. I immediately sent another email admitting my stupidity, then Hugh and I prayed that Sarah wouldn't hate us for all time.

But Sarah, being the perpetual good sport she is, emailed back that after about twenty minutes of yelling at the top of her lungs and banging on the gate, she decided to leave the coffee maker along with some maps of Quito and surrounding areas with the indigenous woman who ran the little mercado (market) down the street from us. The young woman told her she knew who we were.

In Quito less than a week and we already had a reputation!

Day Three Part Two: A New Friend and
More Shower Woes

Funny how things work out. Had we not missed Sarah that day we might not have ever met María.

When we went down the street to collect our coffee maker and maps we decided to buy a few fresh veggies from the indigenous woman while we were there. We filled our bag with about $5.00 worth of veggies, fruit, and rice then handed the woman, who was dressed in a traditional straight-lined black skirt and embroidered shirt, a twenty dollar bill. She said something we couldn't understand and shook her head. Hugh shoved the greenback at her, but she refused to take it. Huh?

About that time someone said, "Can I help you?"

English never sounded so good.

We turned around to see a short-haired Ecuadorian woman in a navy blue A-frame skirt and a colorful blouse. She explained to us that the shopkeeper couldn't (or wouldn't) make change for such a large bill. We dug around in our pockets but only came up with about a dollar. Our new friend pulled $4.00 out of her coin purse and handed it to the shopkeeper. We asked her how we could pay her back, but she just waved her hand and said we would see each other again. Somehow, we believed her.

Our new friend, María, had a sister who married a man from Texas twenty years earlier and now lived in the states. María had spent a lot of time with her sister in Texas, where, according to her, they speak 'Texan.' She was happy to help us because she knew she would be able to practice her English with us. We were fine with that.

Having money but not being able to use it became a common theme for us those first few weeks. Ecuadorians do not like big bills and always ask for exact change. They *hate* making change, and will even lose a sale if it means they get to keep their change. Some Gringo paying with a twenty could wipe out all the change the shop owner has that day.

To dig out of an economic crisis in the 1990s Ecuador basically saved its economy by ditching their currency, the Sucre, and adopting the American dollar. They can mint their own coins, but not paper money. Ever wonder where all the $1.00 coins we didn't want went? They went to Ecuador.

This is one reason Ecuador encourages people from the states to retire there. Retired expats bring their dollars but don't take jobs away from Ecuadorian citizens. We understood this, but always having small bills and change was something we would have to get used to. In the states, we are always trying to get rid of our change, but in Ecuador, change is more precious than gold.

Earlier in the day Hugh had painstakingly penned a letter in Spanish (thank goodness for English/Spanish dictionaries and online translators) to Patricio alerting him to the fact that our shower drain was clogged (the shower saga continued). The young man wasn't home so we had to leave the letter in his locked door grate.

Not only do Ecuadorians triple lock their front gates, they also reinforce all the doors in their buildings (except ours, of course) with an iron grate door that is double locked when they are away from home. In Ecuador, it is not uncommon for several generations to live together in one building, so Patricio and his family lived in the compound with his mother, sister, and some uncles. And, even though they were family they still locked their doors and grates.

When we returned home from the mercado that afternoon, Nora Landlady met us in the hall and asked if we were going to be home for awhile. She read the note we left for her son, called the plumbers, and was expecting them anytime. So, four hours later, at about 8:00 that evening (as we were sitting down to dinner) the plumbers arrived. Not great timing, but I would do about anything to avoid another shower fiasco.

The plumbers worked and worked, scratched their

chins, and worked some more. The problem ended up being a ginormous clump of hair, which didn't make for good dinner conversation, but at least we could once again use the Frankenstein shower.

Later that evening, we met Diana, Nora's daughter (seems Ecuadorians have no problem knocking on your door at 10:00 at night). Diana was the one who had put the ad on the internet for the 'fully furnished' apartment and was the person Sarah had originally spoken with about us renting it.

She was a pretty young woman, with long, light brown curly hair. She was expecting her first child, and she and her boyfriend were setting up one of the apartments in the compound for their upcoming family unit.

In their first conversation, Diana freaked when Sarah told her we had a cat. That was almost a deal breaker. Ecuadorians are crazy for their dogs but haven't caught on yet to the subtle joys of feline companionship. Sure enough, Diana told us (while scrunching up her little button nose) that her family had had a couple of dogs over the years, but *never* a cat. Thankfully, Triplet was on her best behavior and by the time Diana left she made a grand proclamation that our cat was very pretty. She didn't want to touch our three-legged kitty extraordinaire, mind you, but at least she could be in the same room with nuestra gata without having a panic attack.

That day we met Visa Nora, got a real coffee maker,

made a new friend, and had a drain cleaned. Not bad for our third day in Ecuador!

Day Four: A Growing Pile of Laundry and the Trilingual Angi

We woke up to Nora Landlady and little Camila knocking on our door. They brought us more kitchen supplies and three Christmas coffee mugs, one of which we turned into a pen/pencil holder. It was nice to finally have, not only brewed coffee but actual coffee mugs to put it in. This gave Camila another opportunity to pet Triplet, causing her to exclaim, "La gata es muy suave!" I thought we might make cat people out of them yet!

Later that morning, we saw Patricio on the roof with his wife hanging laundry. Quito is a very colorful city along the roof lines because most people hang their laundry out on the roof to dry. Seeing the young couple with their laundry that morning reminded us that we had a growing pile of dirty laundry on our closet floor that needed to be addressed.

Now I don't have a problem with hanging clothes out to dry, but I do have a problem with washing them in the sink with no hot water. So Hugh asked Patricio where the nearest laundry was and he said, "I can go show you now!"

Sofia gave her husband the evil eye, so Hugh said, "Thanks, but it's not an emergency. Maybe we can go when you aren't so busy." Sofia nodded in agreement.

Thirty minutes later, Patricio appeared at our door with a hand drawn map to a laundry business down the street. Do-it-yourself coin laundries are rare in Ecuador, so he was trying to direct us to a laundry service. On the map, he had drawn a small rectangle with the word 'home' written in it. It was so sweet. His family was doing their best to make us feel comfortable.

So Hugh and I took off to find the laundry, Patricio's map in hand. We discovered that afternoon that Patricio would never have a career as a cartographer.

Our failed attempt at finding the laundry (even with the sweet map) put us close to the entrance of Bicentennial Park at the old airport location. Since the laundry chore was a bust, we decided to check out the park.

We were greeted at the entrance by brightly colored whirligigs in the shapes of bees and tigers furiously twirling in the wind. The atmosphere was festive with food vendors, kids on bikes, people walking dogs, a climbing wall, long-tailed kites, and lots of games like hopscotch, sack racing, top spinning, and tackle-the-person-with-the-ball (and do *whatever* you have to do to get that ball!). We walked around for awhile, got a cup of fresh fruit, enjoyed the people watching, and decided it wasn't a bad way to spend a Saturday afternoon, even if we were running out of clean underwear.

Then we headed to SuperMaxi, our daily shopping destination. We wanted to knock out the rest of the staples we needed so that maybe, just maybe, we could go a day or two without walking up the hill to the store.

We decided to support the local mercados for our fresh food, so Hugh waited at the gate to the building with our groceries while I popped down the block to the little store run by the indigenous woman. The young lady that was usually there wasn't there that day, but an older woman (her mother, if I had to guess) was there with a little girl.

The woman started speaking to me in rapid-fire Spanish, and I said, "No, no entiendo español muy bien." She smiled at me, and all of a sudden, her speech drastically morphed into a slow, sing-songy hypnotic melody, and like magic, I could understand her! It was so cool. I wondered if there was room in my pocket for her as well.

She started asking me questions, like where was I from, where did I live, was I married, and so on. I was prepared for this because Sarah had told us on our tour that Ecuadorians are very 'friendly' (nosy) people. They stand close to you when speaking, and they are NOT shy about asking you intimate details of your life. Or to be godparents to their children (which is really a financial request).

This reminded me a little bit of living in the south, where the first questions hurled at a stranger are 1) Who are your people?, and 2) What church do you go to?

The little girl in the shop that day was cute in her orange pants and brown top that matched the color of her eyes. She looked to be around five or six. The older woman told me that her granddaughter, Angi, could speak English, so I asked the girl to show me. She smiled and counted to ten in perfect English. I 'oooed' and 'ahhed' and said how 'intelegente' she was.

Then her grandmother prompted her to count to ten in Quichua, an indigenous language that is still spoken in parts of Ecuador. The girl struggled a bit with that request, but with the help of her grandma, she finished with a smile, and proudly said, "Conosco tres idiomas!" I replied that she was, indeed, trilingual. I said my goodbyes and left feeling more optimistic that one day I might actually be able to speak Spanish!

Day Five: A Chicken Dinner

Hugh woke up craving chicken, so on our daily trek to SuperMaxi we got a whole chicken for him to cook for dinner that night. I'm a vegetarian, but I have never had a problem with Hugh eating whatever he wants (as long as I don't have to cook it).

Walking back from the store that morning, we noticed something we hadn't noticed before; the tops of buildings. Some were very colorful and beautiful, some had the ever-present flapping laundry, and one roof had a huge, bright red cross that overlooked the street nearest the old airport.

Until this point, we had been nervous about looking up. You see, the sidewalks in Quito are not in any way, shape, or form level or predictable, and it is not uncommon to come across a gaping chasm out of nowhere.

On top of that, no one in Ecuador curbs their dog (most of the dogs run free since there are no leash laws) so you really have to watch out or you'll be constantly scraping poo off your shoe. By this time, though, we knew the sidewalks a little better and felt confident we could steal the occasional glance up without facing dire consequences.

I made a mental note that day to look up more often. After all, life does not present itself in a straight line laid out carefully in front of your feet. Sometimes you have to look up, or even sideways, to get the whole picture.

That evening, my carnivorous husband gathered plenty of carrots, onions, and celery, and set out to make a chicken dinner fit for a hungry Hugh. He planned to prepare the chicken as he always did back in the states by boiling the 'insides' on the stove for a gravy while the rest of the chicken cooked in the oven.

Hugh began pulling things out of the cavity of the bird and pointed out to me that not only were the liver and heart there, the feet were in there as well. And then, as he pulled the neck out, he noticed that the chicken's head was still attached, beak and all!

In addition to the chicken, we purchased our first bottle of wine to drink with dinner that evening. Wine, like all alcohol, is pretty expensive in Ecuador. For example, in 2013 a bottle of Bacardi rum cost about $85.00. And Scotch, well, fuggedaboudit! The wine we purchased that day was an $8.00 bottle, so we weren't expecting much.

Problem was, not only did we not have wine glasses, we couldn't find our nifty Rabbit wine opener we thought we had brought with us from the states. Luckily, Hugh is a master with a paring knife, so he was able to remove the cork via the knife and his teeth. We were right not to expect much from the wine, but it did make the meal feel a little more normal. Well, as normal as possible considering we drank the wine out of Christmas mugs.

After dinner, we checked the WeatherBug for the seven day forecast in Quito. It called for light winds with a high of 66 and a low of 50 every day, except for Thursday, when it was supposed to get up to an alarming 67. We had been there almost a week with no rain in sight. Of course, we hadn't been through the rainy season yet, but for the time being, we were diggin' the weather!

Day Six: Time to Take Out the Trash

We finally found the 'Clean Machine' laundry that Patricio had drawn on his map. It was only a few blocks from the penthouse so that morning we dropped off our over-stuffed bag of dirty clothes. The loud woman at the counter said the clothes would be ready at 5:00 that afternoon. At least that's what we thought she said.

I had to laugh because when we didn't understand what she said in Spanish she said the same thing again only louder like we were hard of hearing, not hard of comprehending. I made a mental note not to yell in English when the tables were turned.

On our way back to the penthouse that morning we ran into our new friend, María. We knew we would run into her eventually! We paid her back the $4.00 we owed her, and she generously offered to go with us the following day to help us get set up with cell phones. We still had no way of getting in touch with anyone locally, and until that point, it had not been necessary. But the following week we were supposed to hear from Visa Nora about the next phase of our residency visas and we were eager to get that ball rolling.

We also needed to make sure we could reach Sarah. Her husband was being sent to Argentina for a few months and Sarah thought it would be a good opportunity for her teenage daughters to see a different part of the world. I really think it was Sarah who wanted the adventure, but whatever the reason, they were going to rent out their house for four months and Hugh and I thought it might be our ticket out of the penthouse.

Now to a most pressing problem. We had been in the country for almost a week and had absolutely no idea what to do with our trash. Hugh had asked Nora Landlady about it the previous afternoon and she said they put their garbage out on the sidewalk on Mondays, Wednesdays, and Fridays before 8:00.

THREE times a week?

Well, if you lived in Ecuador you would be thankful the garbage was collected that often. Like it is in most other South American countries, you do not put your toilet paper in the toilet when you are in Ecuador. TP goes in a little trash can beside the commode, regardless of whether you go number one or number two.

I know, I know, some people find that gross, but if you don't want a stopped up toilet (we didn't), you just do it. The city's antiquated pipe system simply can't deal with all that paper. It felt strange at first, and honestly, we forgot several times, but before long it was second nature.

Being a Monday, Hugh got up early that sixth day and put the trash on the sidewalk about 7:15. When he got back to the penthouse he commented that he had not seen any other trash out. We checked again after breakfast. No other trash. Ours was the only, lonely trash on the street all day.

We thought we must have misunderstood Nora Landlady's instructions so we asked Patricio for clarification. He said the trash was to go out before 8:00 en la noche! And sure enough, after 7:00 that night the garbage had multiplied, then at 8:45 we heard the trash truck lumbering down the street.

We stopped by our little vegetable mercado after we picked up our laundry that afternoon. Visiting with the women there was something we now looked forward to every day. Little things were becoming very enjoyable, and I wondered if it could be possible that life wasn't so complicated after all. I mean, we got our trash picked up, talked to our new friend, shopped at our favorite mercado, and got our laundry done. We were feeling pretty good about the day and our decision to move to Ecuador.

Day Seven: Toy Phones

We met María early that afternoon on the corner. We were expecting (and planning) to wait, you know, due to 'mañana' time, but she proved to be a bit of an anomaly (a prompt Ecuadorian). Of course, we were ready to get our phones, but we were also looking forward to learning more about our new friend.

We did not have and were not planning on getting a car, so we needed a supervised meet-and-greet with the public transportation system. María proved to be a great guide. Buses are a very popular form of transportation in Ecuador because the fare is only twenty-five cents. Yep, twenty-five cents per person, per ride. And if you are over sixty-five, it's half price!

While the price was right, we noticed there were no maps or marked bus stops, so we had no idea how to find the 'right' bus. Maria said if we stood on this side of the street and took any blue bus it would take us into downtown Quito. And all you have to do to stop a bus in Quito is stick out your hand (not above shoulder height, mind you, or you come across being about as civilized as a baboon) and they will stop and pick you up anywhere. So that's what we did.

The public city buses in Quito were like public city buses anywhere; they were crowded, loud, and reeked of diesel fumes. Diesel fuel cost about a buck a gallon, unleaded about $1.48, and those prices had been stable and virtually unchanged for several years due to government subsidies. Considering how inexpensive that mode of transportation was, we decided to look past the pesky little inconveniences that came with public transit and just get on the bus.

María prompted us when it was time to get off the bus, which was not as easy as it sounds. You see, bus drivers in Ecuador don't believe in full stops. Once you have one foot out the back door and on the ground, that's good enough for them. Ecuadorians are taught this 'exit' skill at a very young age, but we foreigners have to practice. A lot.

We walked a couple of blocks to the Spiral Mall, one of the older malls in Quito, and went up the circular ramp to a small Claro store in the belly of the building. That's where we got little toy phones. Those mobile phones were from a time so far back we couldn't even remember how to turn them on.

There are two major phone carriers in Ecuador, Claro, and Movistar. Instead of buying a monthly plan, most people just load minutes and reload more when they run out. But as soon as the minutes expire, of course, you get cut off and can no longer make calls.

But Sarah told us you could always *receive* calls. In fact, she told us her daughters had taught her that you can always text the person you want to speak with to let them know you are out of minutes and *they* should call *you*. And, indeed, throughout our years in Ecuador, *we* were the ones who always had to call our Ecuadorian friends because they NEVER HAD MINUTES!

Thank goodness María was with us because the girl at the Claro store spoke no English, and although we had been studying Spanish quite a bit, we found out that day how difficult it was to perform a business transaction in a language other than your own.

After our business at the Claro store, we hopped on another bus and went to a newer mall downtown to treat María to some coffee. One of the most popular coffee places in Quito was called the Sweet & Coffee. This was a chain of stores, not unlike Starbucks, where you could get cappuccinos, ice coffees, espressos, as well as sweet desserts and muffins.

I asked María why the name of the establishment was in English. She said it sounded more exotic that way. The coffee they served at the Sweet & Coffee was Ecuadorian, very good, and brewed! We later found this brand of coffee at SuperMaxi and started making it at home in Sarah's coffee maker.

After our coffee, we strolled around the mall, where I was happy to find a paper store that had origami paper (at least it could be used for origami), and Hugh happened across a backgammon game in a toy store on the upper level. We were now all set for more evenings in the penthouse without TV. Did I mention that the penthouse didn't have a television? Good thing we like to read.

We made plans with María for the following week to take a cable car up the side of Volcán Pichincha. Although she had been several times before, she was happy to go again with us. Ecuadorians are very proud of their country and María was happy for the opportunity to show us one of Ecuador's major attractions.

"Be sure to bring sweaters and coats," she warned us. After we got back to the penthouse, we took inventory of all our warm clothes and hoped they would suffice. Because we were moving to the land of 'perpetual spring,' we had not packed many winter clothes. Oh well, how cold could it be?

Day Eight: Our Second Day On the Bus

After getting our initial 'bus legs' with María the day before, Hugh and I felt more confident in our bus navigating abilities so we decided to strike out on our own. We flagged a blue bus and went a little farther into downtown Quito than we had with María. And because we felt more at ease we were able to notice a few things that we had been too overwhelmed to notice the day before.

For instance, every time the bus stopped someone new got on to push their goods. It might be Chicklets, comic books, energy pills, fresh fruit, or coconut water. Some people only got on to beg for money because their Aunt Marta had had surgery and needed to pay her medical bills.

What amazed us was the age of some of these hawkers. One cute, dirty little fellow selling gum couldn't have been more than seven. And the young ones already had that monotone delivery; un-do-lar-man-zan-as-na-ran-jas-un-do-lar-man-zan-as-na-ran-jas-un-do-lar (one dollar apples oranges, one dollar apples oranges) over and over. We saw some of these children being coached by their fathers on the sidewalks while waiting for a bus to come by.

Out of the smudged windows we saw the Quito Bull Ring. Seems that Ecuadorians, at least in the capital, had lost their stomachs for bulls being killed in the ring. In fact, Quito had not hosted a bullfight in over a year. Some of the smaller more rural towns still had the occasional bullfight, but no one knew how long the tradition would stand. It's true that Ecuador is way behind much of the world in most of their policies regarding the treatment of animals and animal rights, but during our time there we felt the wind begin to change a little. Doing away with bullfighting was a monumental cultural shift and one that made this North American girl happy.

We also saw lots of schoolchildren that day. School uniforms are mandatory in Ecuador and range from your basic gray sweatsuits to dark slacks, white shirts, and ties for boys and plaid skirts, long socks, and sweaters for girls. The kids in Quito look a lot like the kids in the rest of the world, you know, girls with too much makeup twirling their hair between their fingers, and boys trying to look mysterious and cool with spiky gelled hair.

The bus took us all the way to the end of the Avenue of the Amazonas, where there is a big public park. It is a lovely place with fruit stands, flowering trees, and colorful artisan vendor booths. We got some fruit and quietly watched the world go by. We saw old barefooted women asking for handouts and filthy boys begging to shine your shoes. We saw couples strolling hand in hand, dogs looking for scraps, businessmen taking a mid-day break, and kids playing on rusty playground equipment that would make parents in the states cringe. The kids didn't seem to mind the rust. Or the concrete.

And we saw babies. Lots of babies. Funny thing was, we rarely heard them. In Ecuador, babies and small children go everywhere their mothers go. Women strap their babies on their backs with a shawl tied under their arm and across their chest (no fancy baby backpacks or strollers) and just go about their daily business. And it's not uncommon to see a mother breastfeeding, well, anywhere. Parents do tend to be on the young side, but they are attentive and we rarely heard a fussy baby our entire time in Ecuador.

When we finally returned to the penthouse that evening Hugh and I realized we were exhausted. It was obvious we hadn't learned to breathe at 9,000 feet yet because the 4th floor walk up was still kicking our butts. And I think we had underestimated how grueling the preparation for this adventure had really been. But we had made it past the one week mark, and that was a big win in our book.

Day Nine: Old Town

Since we had become bus pros, we decided to visit Old Town, the historical heartbeat of the country where the presidential palace and many of the government buildings are located. The streets are narrow and cobblestone and often have only a fragment of a sidewalk attached. Many of the streets are one-way, which is fine until two one-way streets meet head-on and have to merge until they have an opportunity to turn into other one-way streets.

The historic section of Quito is very steep, and considering we were still acclimating ourselves to the climate, we took our time and walked slowly enough so that we could gawk and stare at the interesting architecture that engulfed us. Old Town Quito has a quaint beauty and a certain flavor that I've not tasted in any other city.

On our tour we came to this section of town to see the changing of the guard ceremony. Every Monday, el presidente, el vicepresidente, y los dignitarios del día appear on the balcony of the presidential palace and preside over the changing of the guards.

Talk about patriotic pomp and circumstance! Brass ensembles, the raising of the Ecuadorian flag, men in full regalia on dancing horses, and lots of people selling hats, t-shirts, and ice-cream (not to mention several opposing political parties with bullhorns and banners) combine to create a carnival-like atmosphere.

It was a lot of fun to watch on our tour the previous year, but, unfortunately, we were there on the wrong day that week. We hoped we would be able to attend at least once while we were living in the capital.

Right near the government section of town, at the very top of one of the steepest hills, is La Basílica del Voto Nacional. This cathedral, the tallest in Ecuador, was begun in 1892 and is still not finished. I think the Ecuadorians have made peace with that fact and are in no hurry to finish.

The gargoyles that line the roof of the Basílica are not your run-of-the-mill scary-monster-type gargoyles. A menagerie of native animals (turtles, iguanas, monkeys, bears, and armadillos, to name a few) hover over the downspouts, and although the inside of the cathedral was spectacular, it was the sight of those animals that made climbing that horrid hill worthwhile.

After wandering the streets for awhile, we came across a cute little coffee shop, 'Luz de Vida Cafeteria.' We enjoyed a delicious cup of Ecuadorian coffee (brewed, thank you), and then the owner, a short, enthusiastic man (who was happy to practice his English) took our picture to put on his Facebook page. Sure enough, we checked a few days later and there we were with big silly grins, our coffee cups lifted in a toast. We 'liked' his page and hoped we would be able to visit him again soon.

Books are very expensive in Ecuador so we were happy to see a used bookstore down the street from the coffee shop nestled in between a sewing shop and a shoe repair closet. OK, technically it was a shoe repair *shop*, but 'closet' is a more accurate description.

We found a lot of translated-into-Spanish classics but settled instead on a couple of kid's books 1) because we were on about a pre-K level in our Spanish studies, and 2) because the larger of the two books had native fables we thought might be interesting. Turned out even *those* books were beyond us at that moment. I was beginning to feel my goal of becoming fluent in Spanish in a year's time was a bit too ambitious.

It was getting late, so we took our first trolley ride back to the Avenue of the Amazonas where we could catch a bus back to the penthouse. We felt like sardines in the trolley it was so packed, but at least we didn't have to choke on diesel fumes.

Back on the familiar Avenue, we bumped into a guy named William Flores, although the taped-over name on his business card stated Wilians Flores. Guess he wasn't sure of the spelling. Here was another Ecuadorian that overheard us speak English and saw an opportunity to practice his. He walked with us several blocks, gave us his card, then disappeared down a side street.

One thing we had noticed on our other forays down the Avenue was a disproportionate number of karaoke bars. We were a bit cautious because we had learned the previous year on our tour that in Ecuador, a 'motel' is not really a motel, and a 'nightclub' is definitely NOT a nightclub. If you want to know what these things actually are, you'll have to take the tour!

We decided to forgo the karaoke joints until we could figure out if they really were places where drunk people made fools of themselves singing 'Hey Jude' and 'Love Shack.'

We opted instead to stop in a little bar that advertised a small selection of craft beer. They weren't kidding about the small selection; you could order red or black. The gringo bar was owned by a very large Belgian dude, Léo, that, if rumor was correct, spoke eight languages. I slyly shoved my baby Spanish books under my legs while sitting on the barstool.

We relaxed with our red and black beers and met a couple of interesting fellows. One was a Canadian who had moved to Ecuador a couple of decades ago. We would go on to meet *lots* of Canadians during our time in South America, more than I ever met in the states.

The other guy was a recently retired professor of botany from Marshall University in West Virginia. He had gotten to know Ecuador through his research. The professor traveled to South America every couple of years and embeded himself with an indigenous group somewhere in the Amazon for a few months at a time to study how the tribe used native plants to treat certain illnesses. He said he was fortunate he hadn't become a shrunken head yet. I laughed, but he was serious. Gulp.

The bus ride home was a long one, or maybe it just seemed that way because the sun was going down, we were tired, and the diesel fumes were especially overpowering that evening. After we got back to the penthouse we made a quick dinner and turned in early. We wanted to be rested for the following day, the day we would make our first visit to the immigration office with Visa Nora.

Day Ten: About That Lunch...

The morning of day ten we got up extra early so that we would be ready for Visa Nora. We had NO idea when she was coming by to pick us up, which I'll admit, was a bit frustrating. I mean, who does business that way? We had no choice but to wait.

So we waited, and we waited. We waited some more. Then, right as we were sitting down to lunch the lovely Sofia knocked on the door. Yep, someone was there to see us.

We left our lunch on the table, grabbed our passports, and rushed down to meet Visa Nora. She had with her a gentleman from Texas, Ron, whom she had also been helping obtain residency. His papers had just been approved, so we felt a little more confident Visa Nora might be able to deliver, after all. He was going with us to the immigration office to pick up his newly stamped passport and apply for his cedula (Ecuador's national ID card), while we were just hoping to get a file started.

It is with a cedula that retirees receive their benefits, like half price transportation (that even includes airline tickets booked within the country to anywhere in the world!), discounts on museums and shows, and a total refund of the VA tax. The cedula is what you want, but you have to get your residency first.

After driving into the center of town, Visa Nora decided to drop her car off at the carwash to have it cleaned. Seems it's easier (and sometimes cheaper) to have your car washed than it is to find a parking place.

We crossed the street to the immigration office and took a number. Of course, the person we needed to see was out to lunch (which reminded me of *my* lunch sitting on the table back at the penthouse), but Ron was able to get his business taken care of. Felicidades, Cowboy Ron, newest resident of Ecuador!

Hugh and I didn't accomplish much that day at the immigration office, but we were able to get confirmation that we had adequate days left on our tourist visas to get the process started. If we got close to running out of our remaining seventy-nine days, we could file for an extension. Visa Nora swore that would not be a problem; I hoped it wouldn't take nearly that long.

Then we headed over to the notary's office to drop off our translated papers to be notarized. Being a notary in Ecuador is a pretty big deal. You have to invest upwards of $100,000.00 to get licensed (which is an *impossible* amount of money for most Ecuadorians) but people know they will make all that money back and lots more, usually within six to nine months. *Everything* has to be notarized in Ecuador, and notaries know it. They are responsible for title searches and other things that lawyers usually take care of in the states, and they have no problem charging a hefty sum for their services. They stay BUSY.

We handed our passports over to Visa Nora (always a little nerve racking to part with your passport in a foreign country) and she disappeared. We waited. And we waited some more. Cowboy Ron was still with us so he entertained us with his travel adventures while we waited, but no amount of amusing entertainment could mask the fact that we waited a looooooong time. Then, just as I began wondering how long it took a person to die of starvation, Visa Nora reappeared, asked us to sign a few papers, and poof! Just like that, we were done with our business for the day.

Back at the carwash, a shaggy-haired attendant overheard us speaking English, so, of course, he wanted to squeeze in a little practice with us. I didn't mind. It's nice to be able to share your language, and this young man could hardly contain his excitement for the opportunity to speak with native English speakers.

When we left the carwash we asked Visa Nora if she could drop us off at the MegaMaxi store. We needed to get our permanent SuperMaxi card (a store loyalty card) as well as a bigger litter box for Triplet, a rug for her to scratch on, and a haba (case) of beer. Other than our red and black craft beer at the Gringo bar, we had not had any beer since we had arrived all those long days ago, and we were, well, thirsty.

Visa Nora worried that we would have trouble finding the right bus to get us back to the penthouse, but we had already taken care of that. Our friend, Bob, was going to pick us up.

We met Bob on our scouting tour the previous year. He, like Sarah, had been in the Peace Corps and had fallen in love with an Ecuadorian while he was stationed in the country. Bob and his wife owned some coffee and avocado farms north of Quito and they were gracious hosts to our tour group when we were passing through that part of the country.

Bob had managed to trash his iPhone earlier in the year, so his son (who was living in the states at the time) mailed us a new phone before we moved to take to his father. Our mission was to get that phone into Bob's hands before we ended up losing (or breaking) it!

If you ever visit someone who lives abroad you should be prepared to take stuff to them. Gringos in Ecuador rely on human mules to get things they need because 1) Ecuador is kind of a 'basics' only country, so if your life depends on having name brand or exotic products (think Skippy peanut butter, Estee Lauder face cream, or Indian spices) you are out of luck, and 2) there is no mail service to speak of.

Wait, no mail service? Hard to wrap your head around, right? And while you can 'technically' receive mail in Ecuador the truth is most of the time the boxes arrive empty, having been pilfered along the way. *And* you have to pay for the privilege of picking your mail up. *And* the mail can't weigh over four pounds. Sometimes the particulars change, but it is always difficult and costly to receive mail in Ecuador, so it's best to avoid the postal service altogether if possible.

So Bob picked us up at the MegaMaxi that afternoon, which sure beat trying to catch a bus with a haba of brewskis! He got his new iPhone, and we were finally able to eat lunch at 7:00 that evening.

Days Eleven ~ Twenty

Day Eleven: Sarah's Casita

Hugh and I had been in the habit of waking with the sun in the states, which would vary depending on the time of year and whether or not we were observing daylight savings time. But in Ecuador, waking with the sun meant we woke up at 6:00 every morning. At the equator, the sun always rises and sets at the same time everyday, roughly 6:00 in the morning and 6:00 in the evening. And, no, Ecuador has no use for daylight savings time!

So we woke early on day eleven, the day that would take us to Conocoto to see Sarah's 'casita,' or little house. Ecuadorians add 'ita' or 'ito' to the end of names as an endearment, like mamacita, Carlosito, Sofita, etc. But they also add the suffix to words like 'house' and 'dollar.' Many times on the bus we heard, "Pero solo un dolarito!" which means, "But it only costs a tiny, little dollar!"

We met Sarah at Parque Carolina that morning. She said before she took us to see her house she needed to deliver some packets of material for her upcoming tour, so we went with her to the hostel where her next group would be staying their first night in Ecuador. She told us she and Jonathan, her business partner, had cranked things up a bit since our tour.

Our tour group had stayed at a plain hostel (a bed in your room and nothing else) run by a young family the first night of our tour, which was fine with us. But for the following tours, Sarah booked rooms in fancier hostels and kicked the first night off with a wine and cheese reception. Wine. And CHEESE! Humph. I tried not to sulk.

The place Sarah had booked was amazing. Built in the 1800s for a wealthy family, the hostel looked like a museum, with a lot of bold contemporary art mixed in among more traditional paintings, impossibly wide scalloped crown molding, rich, deeply colored wool rugs, and a canopy bed in every room. Sarah said the food was gourmet and there was always hot water in the showers (now that was rubbing it in don't you think?). She and Jonathan had decided to 'ease' the tour group into a more realistic version of the country a little at a time. We understood, but I sure wished I had a shot at one of those showers!

Then we were off to Conocoto, Sarah pointing out historical landmarks and road signs on the way (always the tour guide), trying to get us familiar with that part of the country in case we decided to rent her house while she and her family were in Argentina. I think she felt sorry for us in our tiny little penthouse with the Frankenstein shower and thought her casita might be a viable option for us until we could figure out what to do next. Sarah was like that, always trying to find a way to make others more comfortable and happy. I was still trying to figure out how to fit her in my pocket.

Sarah received a settlement when she retired (after twenty years) from the Peace Corps, and she and her husband decided to use the money to build their dream house. They also invested well by building several packed earth 'cottages' on their property that they rented to passersby.

Her two story casita was in the valley on a beautiful piece of land that faced the mountains. The house was airy, colorful, fun, and we could tell that she, her husband, and their three daughters had filled the house with love and many warm memories. Hugh and I could definitely see ourselves living there for a few months until we figured something else out. Plus, it had five bedrooms, so we would have plenty of room if my parents and our friend, Bo, visited like they were planning to later that year.

Sarah told us a little about her renters on the drive that morning and we met several of them that day. The first couple we met was from the Ukraine and spoke Spanish, but not much English, so there wasn't much for us to talk about.

The second couple we met was from Oregon. Sarah had told us they were nice people, but she wished they would socialize more. She indicated they only went to town once a week to shop for groceries, but other than that they were pretty reclusive.

Sarah knocked on Dave and Susanne's door and they invited us in. We chatted for a while and compared the various card and board games we either did or did not have in common, as well as the differences between Oregon and South Carolina. They offered to give us a tour of their cottage, which was charming and the perfect size for a retired couple.

About ten minutes after we returned to Sarah's the power flickered, then went out completely. It did not return in five minutes. Or ten. After about twenty minutes, Dave, from next door, came over to see if Sarah knew anything about the power being out.

While Sarah tried to reach the power company on the phone, Hugh and I slipped into host/hostess mode and offered Dave some wine, which he gladly accepted. It was a relaxing afternoon, and we thought Dave and Susanne were pretty friendly after all, even if they didn't get out much.

If we couldn't get anything else worked out soon we felt confident that Conocoto would be a good place for us to settle down for awhile.

We didn't know it at the time, but life would lead us in another direction.

Day Twelve: Mean Wind and Rusty Pipes

We woke up early that Sunday and spent a good part of the morning studying Spanish. Do you remember what it was like as a child being in a room full of adults and only picking out a word or two of what they said? That's how I felt when we were out and about in Quito those first weeks. I was excited when I recognized a word here or there, but I still didn't have a clue what the Spanish speaker was saying. Yes, it was time to buckle down and get serious about learning our new language.

Sundays had always been 'pancake day' back in the states. I love making pancakes from scratch, sometimes with fresh fruit, sometimes with pecans or walnuts, and always with a tiny hint of cinnamon. My problem in continuing our weekend pancake tradition in Quito was that Ecuador doesn't sell baking soda.

Wait. Let me take that back. They sell baking soda in super small quantities at the pharmacy. No, they don't sell baking soda at the grocery store. Why? Well, since Ecuador borders Colombia it seems the Ecuadorian government doesn't want baking soda being used to cut cocaine in their country.

Have you ever tried to bake without baking soda? I'm here to tell you, it ain't pretty.

On one of our trips to SuperMaxi we saw a pancake mix, so we decided to try it. Now considering we only had one small skillet and I had to cook the flapjacks one at a time they turned out all right, I guess. The pancakes were a bit taller, poofier, and chewier than the ones I made back home in South Carolina, but they weren't bad.

I had to accept that learning to cook at such a high altitude would take some getting used to. I had *no idea* of the upcoming challenges we would face in the cooking department, but for the time being, we were making out all right, and I was confident we wouldn't starve.

Sarah had warned us that we were approaching the windy season in Quito, and that morning we got our first taste of what that meant. The non-energy efficient single pane windows in the penthouse shook violently and we felt gusts of wind no matter where we were in the penthouse. Yes, *in* the penthouse. Triplet was not impressed. All day, all night, such wind!

Later in the afternoon, I Skyped with my good friend, Joyce. It was only July, and already that year she had lost her mother, her uncle, her sweet doggie, and her priest. I thought about the times I would not be there to console friends and family during their times of loss or to celebrate with them during their times of joy and success.

Not all costs of moving abroad can be easily factored in during the initial decision-making process. After all, knowing something and living something are two different things.

After I finished my call with Joyce I realized how much I missed my piano (Joyce had been one of my piano students, as well as a friend). But I had a digital piano coming via a shipping container our friends Max and Stephanie were having delivered to Ecuador, so I tried not to get too bummed.

Hugh and I met Max and Stephanie on our tour the previous year. They were also considering a move to Ecuador at that time, and we had to laugh because come to find out, they only lived about twenty miles away from us in the states. We had to go to the southern hemisphere to meet our neighbors!

Max and Stephanie were already in Ecuador, having moved to the lovely old city of Cuenca earlier in the year, but their container had not arrived yet. I knew I would have to wait for my piano once we arrived in Ecuador, so I decided to take up the recorder because it was easy to slip into my carry-on bag. I was having fun with my new instrument and it at least kept me in touch with music, but I don't think Triplet enjoyed listening to me practice very much.

Whenever I got my recorder out she went and hid in the Frankenstein shower. Everyone's a critic.

When I went to our little shotgun kitchen that evening to start dinner, I slipped on a puddle of water in the middle of the floor. Not a good sign.

After a preemptive sigh, Hugh opened the door under the sink, and there it was. The ugly truth. The pipe under the kitchen sink had not just come undone but had rusted straight through. So Hugh went downstairs to report to Nora Landlady the new plumbing challenge in the penthouse, but being domingo (Sunday), there was nothing she could do. We would have to wait, which was something we were getting good at.

Day Thirteen Part One: The Little Cab That Couldn't

After having slept with a piece of cardboard shoved between the door and jamb to keep the door from rattling all night from the wind, we were happy to wake the next morning to a much quieter environment. We thought we would have to postpone our planned play-date with María to Volcán Pichincha because of the wind, but it looked like we would be able to go after all!

We met María at the corner at 8:00 that morning and caught our favorite blue bus. She insisted on treating us to breakfast at a place she knew downtown that specialized in 'American Style' cuisine. I'd say it was 'American-ish,' but she was sweet to offer and we enjoyed spending time with her. Hugh had bacon and eggs (with the yolks runny, of course) and I had a huge bowl of fresh fruit with granola and yogurt. The crusty bread was warm and the mermelada de mora (blackberry marmalade) had been made that morning.

Hugh and I were secretly dreading the coffee, thinking it would be instant. Hugh ordered café con leche (coffee with milk) thinking the milk would mask the instant flavor, but instead of bringing him instant coffee with cream on the side our server brought him a cup of hot milk along with a little syrup dispenser that contained 'essence' of coffee. He could then control the strength of the coffee by how much syrup he poured in the milk. He said it wasn't bad! I don't like milk in my coffee so I got the café con agua (coffee with water), which meant I got the dreaded instant concoction, but honestly, everything else was so good, I hardly noticed. And, of course, the waitress got a chance to practice her English.

After breakfast, María suggested we find out how much a cab would be to the teleférico (the lift that takes you up to the top of the volcano) because it would take us several bus rides and a big chunk of time to get there. So we stopped a cab to ask.

We let María do the talking because gringos always get charged more than Ecuadorians. At that time in Quito you had to negotiate prices in advance with cab drivers because they didn't use meters. What, no meters? Nope, no meters. But María did a great job and secured us a cab ride across town for $2.00. It would have cost the three of us at least twice that on the bus and would have taken us four times as long to get there, so we were happy.

We zipped across town with no problems until we got to the cable car entrance where there was a steep hill to get to the ticket office. The cab stuttered, the cab sputtered, then it choked and lurched before conking out completely. The cabbie shyly smiled and said he might, just maybe, be out of gas. Are you kidding me!?!

So we got out of the cab, paid the driver his lousy two bucks, and started huffin' up the side of the mountain. We're talkin' at least three-quarters of a mile straight up. STRAIGHT UP at 15,000 feet. I mean, come on, I hadn't learned to breath at 9,000 feet yet!

Now, I tend to be a glass-half-full type of person, but none of us could find a silver lining in having to climb that ghastly hill. We couldn't even *pretend* it was funny.

We (barely) survived the death march and purchased our tickets for the teleférico. Then a teen in an orange reflective vest led us to a tiny orange cable car he claimed could hold up to six people. This thing looked like a toy and I couldn't see how my six foot plus husband was going to fit in there with five other people, but it worked out. The others in the car with us ended up being a below-average size South American couple, so Hugh had plenty of room for his legs after all. María engaged the pair in conversation and found out they were both trombone players. What? Yeah, professional trombone players. From Argentina.

On the way up the mountain we occasionally passed cars en route back down. Everybody in our car would wave to the descending passengers, which made me feel a little silly, but I did it anyway because I didn't want to come across as a stick-in-the-mud sour-puss. I was a bit scared of the height, you see, but I didn't want to spoil everyone's fun.

After what seemed like three hours to me (really only twenty minutes, más o menos) we finally got to the top, and there we were, standing on this awesome mountain, one of the highest in Ecuador. It was not just cold, it was get-under-your-skin-in-two-seconds-flat cold. Our exposed faces were assaulted by what felt like tiny icy daggers and I wondered how long it would take for hypothermia to set in. No wonder María had insisted on giving us extra hats and scarves that morning.

The view was, well, how can you assign mere words to such a breathtaking sight? Hugh and I both took some pictures, but after a while, we decided to just enjoy the moment. Pictures would never be able to adequately depict the raw, vast, and perfect beauty of what we saw that morning so we became as still as we could (in the breezy sub-freezing weather) and let the magnificence wash over us.

Coming down the mountain was not nearly as fun as going up because you could see exactly how high you were and how far there was still to travel in that small, wobbly cable car. It didn't help matters that about halfway down the car hiccuped to a complete stop, leaving us dangling three hundred feet over the side of a volcano.

I was not happy, to say the least, and begged Hugh not to move because that made the car sway. He found that funny and proceeded to 'rock the boat' with a little flick here and a little flick there, which amused María. Fortunately, we were only stranded for about ten minutes, but I think those were the longest ten minutes of my life.

Finally back on suelo firme, María informed us that she had some time left before her next obligation, so did we want to do anything else? Of course, we did! She suggested the botanical gardens in Parque Carolina right off the Amazonas Avenue, so we held out our hands and caught the next blue bus.

Day Thirteen Part Two: The Carnivores

On our tour the previous fall, Hugh and I had been amazed at the abundance of cacti in the Andes. I always associated 'cacti' with the desert, but the botanical gardens in Parque Carolina had a whole section of different 'typos de cacti,' many in full, bright chromatic bloom. Some of those pricklers dwarfed Hugh (which was a little freaky), but some were smaller than my pinkie finger.

Everywhere we wandered that afternoon we came across these funky, green, glow-in-the-dark, iridescent-looking hummingbirds that flitted, darted, and buzzed over our heads. They were about three times the size of the hummers we had back in of South Carolina, like hummers on steroids. We had fun watching them dive through the small waterfalls in the park and, although there were many varieties of flowers on exhibit, they seemed to prefer the nectar from the purple ones.

About halfway through the park we came to an eerie greenhouse creepily dedicated to the 'carnivores.' I wondered what they fed those plants because one of the things I loved about living at such a high altitude was the absence of bugs. I have always been a mosquito magnet, but the only bugs I had seen in Quito up to that point had been three lethargic flies and a few moths that enjoyed taunting Triplet. But the carnivore plants looked happy and well-fed (some were downright nightmarish), so I guess the gardeners knew how to keep them full.

The gardens boasted a large collection of specialty roses, some wearing colors I had never seen on a flower. Come to find out, Ecuador is one of the world's biggest exporters of flowers, particularly roses. The scent in that part of the park was nothing short of bliss. Roses grow year round in Ecuador, and at the many flower markets across the country you will only pay around $3.00 to $5.00 for a dozen roses. That's a pretty cheap way to stay out of the dog house!

María was a most gracious guide, but she had an appointment in another part of town that afternoon, so we thanked her and went our separate ways. It wasn't until we arrived back in our barrio did we remember that we had an inoperable kitchen sink at home, so we decided to grab a late lunch near the penthouse.

We opted for this little pizza joint where we got two huge slices of pizza and some sparkling water for $3.40. Now I don't want to give the impression that *everything* is so affordable in Ecuador, but when it is, it really is.

Day Thirteen Part Three: An Ecuadorian Fix

Back at the penthouse, we waited and waited for Nora Landlady to show up with the plumbers. About 8:30 that night we came to the obvious conclusion they were not coming. Nora Landlady showed up at 9:00 to confirm our suspicions that, indeed, the plumbers would not be fixing our sink that evening. We resigned ourselves to 'mañana' and I hopped in the shower.

Of course, as soon as I lathered my hair there was a knock at the door. The plumbers had shown up after all. At 9:30. In the evening! Luckily, I had my clothes with me in the bathroom so I didn't have to come out in my birthday suit.

After tearing out the offending pipe, the plumbers did a typical 'Ecuadorian fix.' They installed a paper-thin plastic accordion pipe that they 'sort of' shaped to look like a P-trap (Hugh had to reshape it after they left), but we were happy because we could once again use the sink. And, hopefully, we would be gone before it broke again.

I say typical 'Ecuadorian fix' because it is common knowledge that people in Ecuador (and throughout South America) basically patch things over and over (and over) again. They find as many ways possible to get every millimeter of use out of everything: clothes, cars, shoes, roofs, radios, ovens, backpacks, you name it. This is not a bad thing, and we should all be more resourceful and waste less. But sometimes that means things break more often.

Come to find out, this would not be the worst plumbing fix we would encounter. At our next apartment, we also had trouble with the kitchen pipes, this time in the form of a seriously clogged drain. Instead of cleaning out and replacing what needed to be replaced, the plumbers opted to reroute the sink drain pipes to the downspout next to our little balcony through a huge hole they tore through the wall. Our kitchen sink drain water ran out onto the street via the downspout. I kid you not.

We had friends back home in the states who, about this time, were wondering how we could possibly tolerate the sparse and challenging conditions we had encountered so far. How were two adults and a cat peacefully coexisting in a teeny tiny 4th floor walk up with a Frankenstein shower and a dorm sized fridge? No hot water in the kitchen sink? No washing machine? You have to BOIL the water before you drink it? You take buses everywhere? You have to pass through armed guards at the grocery store? How does Hugh get any sleep in that short bed?

All I can say is that Hugh and I had done our research, and nothing that had happened so far surprised us. We were excited about being able to live a life that was flexible and organic for a change, a real day to day life of living in the moment, taking things as they rolled our way, and not worrying so much about the Joneses.

Plus, we happened to enjoy each other's company. We felt light, unencumbered, and were finding delight in things we had never taken the time to notice before. Yes, we were looking forward to getting our paperwork done so we could move on to a more permanent and suitable living situation, but until then we decided to just go with the flow. Oftentimes, though, that would prove to be easier said than done.

Day Fourteen: A Call From Max

To celebrate the end of our first two weeks in Ecuador Hugh and I studied Spanish and trekked up the hill to SuperMaxi. A little anticlimactic, but we did find a bottle of wine at the grocery store that came with a wine glass gratis (free) which meant we wouldn't have to drink wine out of Christmas mugs anymore.

Max called us that afternoon to let us know he saw an interesting apartment for rent in Cuenca on one of the expat gringo websites. These sites are little hubs for expats to trade, buy and sell, advertise, ask questions, you know, an internet bulletin board. He said he would be happy to check it out for us if it was something we thought we might be interested in.

Hugh and I had originally planned on staying in different parts of the country, six months here, four months there, but that was before we decided to bring Triplet along. We thought she had been a good sport so far but didn't want to press our luck, so we wanted to find a more permanent situation. We hadn't really considered Cuenca as an option.

I take that back. Cuenca was the last stop on our tour,

and I can honestly say we fell in love with that city. Cuenca is the 'artistic' capital of Ecuador and is super quaint with cobblestone streets, four rivers, and several universities. Cuenca also has an active symphony and city sponsored art shows and exhibits that attract artists from all over the world. We *loved* Cuenca.

But Cuenca is also one of the most expensive places to live in the country. We felt it would be out of our budget and had marked it off our list of possible places to live in Ecuador.

We reconsidered when Max told us about this awesome two bedroom, two bath apartment located in El Centro (the historic district), furnished, with all utilities, cable TV, and internet included in the price of the rent. Plus, since the apartment didn't come with a washing machine, the deal included the landlady doing our laundry at no extra charge. Wow.

So Hugh emailed the apartment contact, Roberto (who insisted on being called 'Bob'), about the listing and arranged a time for Max to meet him to check it out for us.

We didn't want to get our hopes up, but to celebrate our 'possible' move to Cuenca Hugh opened a bottle of wine with the paring knife (we had procured glasses, but alas, no corkscrew yet) and we enjoyed our vino with a home cooked spaghetti dinner. Things were looking up!

Day Fifteen: Waiting on Visa Nora Part One

The first day of week three was a do-nothing-but-wait-on-Visa-Nora day. The notary had supposedly finished our paperwork, so Visa Nora was to fetch the papers then swing by to pick us up and take us to the immigration office to officially file our papers and get a case number. We thought we would hear from her that morning, but not a peep.

On a positive note, Max called to say that he thought the Cuenca apartment would be a good fit for us. It was at the end of a dead end street so it would be quiet, it had a small balcony so Triplet could get some fresh air, and it had a nice sized kitchen with all the appliances you could hope for (microwave, toaster oven, and a *regular* sized refrigerator, thank you very much!). And no Frankenstein shower. Yay! We decided then and there to move to Cuenca as soon as we got our visas.

We weren't looking forward to telling Sarah about our decision to move to Cuenca after we had told her we would probably rent her place for a few months, but we were sure that, not only would she understand, she would be very happy for us. That's just how she is.

So with that taken care of, we got back to the serious business of waiting for Visa Nora. After lunch, Hugh finally called her to see what the holdup was. Nora told us the lawyer who had started the notary process had gone out of town and that only the person who starts the process can finish it. Really!? I wondered what happened if the person who started the process got hit by a big blue bus and *couldn't* finish it. I mean, come on.

Visa Nora said she was going to wait on him to get back to the office that afternoon, and then if we had time, she would come get us and take us to the immigration office. So more waiting.

At 3:45 Nora Landlady knocked on the door to announce that we had a visitor. About damn time. We'd been waiting since 8:00 that morning!

We went downstairs thinking we would be going to the immigration office, but Visa Nora told us the papers still weren't ready. She said the girl at the notary's office promised her the papers would be ready by 5:30 that afternoon, but, unfortunately, immigration stopped giving out numbers at 4:00. So Visa Nora said she would pick up the papers from the notary first thing the next morning and come for us at 11:00 to take us to the immigration office.

So we climbed back up to the penthouse and tried not to get discouraged. At least we didn't have to worry about what we were going to be doing the next day. Sigh.

.

Day Sixteen: Waiting on Visa Nora Part Two

Roberto-Bob, the real estate agent in Cuenca, told Hugh he would be emailing us a contract for the apartment. We would need to print it, sign it, scan it, and send it back as soon as possible, which normally would be no problem, but our printer/scanner was in our box of stuff we had packed in Max and Stephanie's container.

Luckily, Ecuador has no shortage of print and copy shops. We had four to choose from on our block. Finding the one that had someone who spoke English was going to be the challenge.

Then there was the matter of the apartment deposit.

Credit cards are not taken in Ecuador like they are in the states. You can't just give someone your credit card info on the phone (or anywhere, for that matter) because they like CASH. They want to see the green and feel the paper. They like the way money smells.

So we were in Quito and needed to get cash to Cuenca fast. We had decided we would ask María to help us wire the money when Max called and said he would cover us. I don't know who wanted to kiss him more, me or Hugh.

We still had not received the contract, so all we could do was get back to the business of waiting for Visa Nora. Hugh and I took turns looking out over the roof for her because her phone had quit 'working' the previous afternoon, which really meant she was out of minutes. We had been lucky the day before that Nora Landlady had been home to hear all the banging downstairs. Seriously, would it be so difficult for Nora Landlady to install a buzzer in the penthouse?

About noon, Hugh looked over the side of the building and saw Visa Nora. We knew something was wrong when she said she needed to come up.

She had to take a minute to catch her breath, but she was finally able to convey that it looked like she would need an apostilled certified copy of our marriage license after all. This meant she would have to translate the new document and take it *back* to the notary for his approval. Geez. So we turned over the document she had originally said she didn't need, and she said she would be in touch, hopefully, later that evening. We decided not to hold our breath.

However, we did receive the contract from Roberto-Bob later that afternoon, and since our plans with Visa Nora didn't work out we were able to go to the little print shop on the corner to take care of our contract business.

The print shop, like most businesses in Ecuador, was a

family affair. Working that day were the son and daughter (late teens, early twenties) and their mother. This family had lived in the states for a couple of years, so the son spoke English pretty well and understood exactly what we needed to do.

While the young man was helping Hugh, I had a nice little conversation with the Mother (of course, she wanted to only speak English) about the states and Quito and the different parts of Ecuador she thought we would enjoy visiting. After taking almost thirty minutes with us, the grand total was fifty-one cents. No, really. $0.51!!!

Visa Nora called at 9:00 that evening to let us know she did get the document translated and delivered to the notary. She would pick it up the next morning, then swing by to get us. Oh, and by the way, she said, would you like a puppy? We thanked her for the puppy offer but didn't think Triplet would approve of such an addition.

So the visa saga would continue el proximo día...

Day Seventeen Part One: Finally

We knew we wouldn't hear from Visa Nora until later in the morning, so we decided to get some laundry done. We wanted to try this other laundry service we had seen on one of our walks around the barrio. It was a little closer, which meant Hugh didn't have such a long way to carry our sack of clothes. On more than one occasion we felt the stares from our neighbors, and I wondered what they thought about the gringo with the big sack on his back, like Kris Kringle.

Ecuadorians have a distinct way of greeting each other. They give each other a quick peck on the right (always the right!) cheek. That's the greeting we got from Valeria, the young woman at the new laundry. She also insisted on giving us a fresh mandarina (what we would call a tangerine) from the bag she had just purchased off a fruit cart (a bicycle cart with a huge crate on the back and a large multi-colored umbrella sticking out of the handlebars). Of course, we had to speak English with her, but she was sweet and the mandarina was juicy.

On the way back from our new favorite laundry place

we ran into María. She was on her way to deliver a birthday cake to her niece and then she was off to Ibarra for a few days for work. Ibarra is called 'The White City' in Ecuador due to the many white-washed colonial houses. There is an interesting story that when the city was in the throes of the plague in the early 1700s the town's officials began painting the buildings with a white lime mixture to try to stave off the spread of the disease. No one I talked to could verify that, but it's a good story anyway.

I never understood exactly what María's job was, but she did some type of mission work and often traveled to different regions up north and sometimes to the coast, where her father lived. Ecuador's society is predominately Catholic, but María and her family were not. She belonged to some evangelical sect, which was fine with me as long as she didn't try to convert me, which she never did.

We told María our news about moving to Cuenca, and, although she said she would miss us, she seemed pleased that she would have a new place in the country to visit. Even Ecuadorians love Cuenca.

Back at the penthouse we started waiting for Visa Nora again. To our surprise, only two hours passed before she called to let us know she was on the way to the notary's office and would be by to get us right after that. She finally arrived at 12:15 (we felt fortunate it wasn't an all-day wait again), and an hour later we *finally* made it to the immigration office.

Day Seventeen Part Two: The Immigration Office

When we got to the immigration office Visa Nora asked us to wait by the door while she got us a number. We were assigned number 89, but they were only on number 78, so Visa Nora suggested we go grab an almuerzo.

An almuerzo is a fixed price lunch in Ecuador that usually costs between $1.50 and $3.50. It includes fresh fruit juice, some type of soup, a plate of rice and beans with either chicken or beef (fish if you are on the coast), sometimes a salad, and usually a small piece of cake or fruit for dessert.

I was concerned about leaving the immigration office because I *hated* the thought of missing our number being called, but Visa Nora assured me we would be waiting the better part of the afternoon. Great. Something to look forward to.

There was a small hostel beside the immigration office that served meals, so Visa Nora took us there. Being vegetarian, I was worried that it would be difficult for me to find something to eat because usually places that serve almuerzos only serve almuerzos, meaning you can't order off a menu. But Visa Nora was a regular there and knew the owner, so she was able to ask for a few substitutions and I got more than enough to eat that afternoon.

Most businesses in Ecuador have televisions on all the time. It wouldn't do to miss a fútbol (soccer) game, and there is almost always a soccer game being televised from somewhere in the world. But that day the TV was set on the news.

The big news of the day was still soccer related, however. The station was playing wall to wall coverage of a popular Ecuadorian soccer player's funeral. He had been in his late twenties and died suddenly of a heart attack a couple of days earlier. Soccer is HUGE in Ecuador, so the entire country was mesmerized by this story. Visa Nora watched reverently as the Ecuadorian flag was draped over his coffin.

I should not have been concerned because we got back to the Immigration office with plenty of time left to wait. So I took the opportunity to study some Spanish vocabulary note cards I had gotten in the habit of carrying around with me, and Hugh played his favorite phone game, Jewels (I joke about him always playing with his jewels). After going through the cards about seven times, I turned to people watching.

I could have been at the DMV back home. There was a little dude, about five, running around with his ADD self, weaving between the rows of strangers and making "brum brum" sounds for his toy car. A couple of 'tweens' were flirting two rows in front of us, all googly eyed and giggly, and a pimply older teen was obviously humiliated by having to sit between his geeky parents. A young mother was breastfeeding on the back row while the man beside her couldn't stop yawning. Come to think of it, everyone looked bored (except the kid with the toy car).

After about an hour we saw a half dozen fair-haired gringas go into a special office, where, we assumed, they were going to pick up their final papers. I desperately wanted to see the inside of that office. I wanted to *be* one of those gringas that afternoon and put this part of the process behind me, but, to be fair, they had already paid their dues and deserved what they got in that room.

All we could do that day was file our petition and get a case number, which is, after all, a pretty big thing. I would have to be patient. Besides, we managed to accomplish our mission that day. We had a case number! Whoo-hoo!

So the third day was the charm waiting for Visa Nora. She delivered us back to the penthouse and promised she would follow up with the people she knew in the office. If you don't keep showing up, she said, your file slips down to the bottom of the pile and you could be in limbo for months.

Something about that made me a little nervous. She assured us she would stay on top of things, and we would hear something in two or three weeks. And with that, she drove off.

All we could do now was settle in for a few more weeks of waiting.

Day Eighteen Part One: Serenades and a Market

Visa Nora told us about a big weekend market called 'Iña Quito' where alcohol was much cheaper than at SuperMaxi. That did it. We knew we had to check it out. So after breakfast, we hopped on our first blue bus of the day.

The bus ride began like all others, kind of crowded and already smelling of diesel. At the second stop, a young woman with curly hair and a red oblong box got on the bus. She stood at the front of the bus and muttered a few words, not really loud enough for anyone to understand. Then she turned on the 'box,' which was a mini karaoke machine, and started belting out a popular Shakira song. Poor girl didn't have much of a voice, and I'm being kind. I was almost willing to give her a tip if she would promise to use it for singing lessons. Luckily, our first stop appeared quickly.

When we got on the next bus we had to squeeze past two men who were raising the rafters with a couple of guitars and a pan flute. The music was traditional, loud, and fun. And the singing wasn't bad. We hated to get off the bus that time.

We thought the serenading was over, but then, right outside the market, we walked by a young woman standing on a table; she was singing a love song (a cappella, mind you) to her boyfriend as a dozen men played cards for money on the sidewalk. We voted her best voice of the day.

The Iña Quito market was comprehensive, to say the least. Little closet sized tiendas that sold everything from booze to flowers to paper towels and gummy bears lined the perimeter of the market. Inside, the stands were open and abutted to each other so that we weren't sure where one ended and the next began.

The main section was all fruits and vegetables, with rows and rows of produce piled so high it almost touched the ceiling in places. I'll admit, we were a bit overwhelmed. With so much food staring at you, how do you know who to go to? Why buy from this person and not that one over there? I mean, everyone was selling the same types of vegetables, so what makes a person stop at this little produce stand here and not that one there?

While I was pondering the complexity of the situation, Hugh discovered the lunch area off to the side of the main market. Two long lines of all types of food imaginable stretched in front of us as far as we could see. Enormous pots of soup (I swear I have never seen pots that big), huge rectangular containers of potatoes and onions, other large pans with rice and beans, and bowl after bowl of fresh fruit, on and on, more and more food. Down toward the end of the second row a whole pig was being chopped up for bar-b-q. At least he didn't have an apple in his mouth like the cooked pigs on the side of the road did.

Then there was the meat section of the market. Sides of beef hung in the open air, along with pig heads, cow tongues (are they really that big?), skinned rabbits, sausages of all shapes, colors and sizes, plucked chickens, slabs of lamb, goat meat, and marinaded cuy (hate to be the one to tell you, but cuy is guinea pig and Ecuadorians eat them). I'll admit this vegetarian wanted to vomit.

I was confident I would have better luck getting down the seafood aisle. I, on occasion, will eat seafood and had actually developed a taste for crab legs before we moved. So I was happy that one of the first things we saw on the seafood row was a pile of freshwater river crabs tied together in square bundles. The crustaceans were smaller than what I was used to seeing, but they still looked big enough to be worth the work.

Hugh had gone ahead, and when I turned to follow him I heard a strange clicking sound behind me. I looked back at the crabs and they were moving. Click, clickity, click, click, like they were beckoning me to return to them. I will admit it freaked me out a bit.

So while Hugh continued to browse the seafood

selections I headed over to the queso department. We had yet to find a cheese at SuperMaxi that came close to the quality of cheeses we were accustomed to back in the states. We like sharp cheeses, but most of what they offer in Ecuador is a very mild crumbly type of cheese that doesn't want to melt. The grocery store had fifty brands of the same, boring queso.

I did see some goat cheese and cheddar that was marked sharp behind the counter that day, but it didn't look like the señora running the counter had washed her hands in about three weeks, so I passed on the cheese.

SuperMaxi's biggest competitor is Santa María. We had not seen one yet, but when we left the market we noticed one on the corner. Hugh suggested we take a look.

Day Eighteen Part Two: A Pretty Good Day

Hugh's first comment after entering Santa María was, "This store looks like it's more for the people," meaning it was a down-home type of store not geared towards gringos and rich Ecuadorians, like the SuperMaxi stores were.

About thirty kinds of dried beans and almost as many types of rice in big bins lined the first few aisles. The store sold almost everything in bulk, including cereal, gummy worms, and baby diapers. After the grocery section, we came across a big home section that sold tons of plastic 'stuff,' like kitchen utensils, colorful juice pitchers, laundry baskets, flowerpots, and rows and rows of plates and bowls. All that 'stuff,' by the way, was made in China.

One thing we had been looking for but hadn't found yet was a large aluminum pot for popping popcorn. Roger, one of our guides from the tour the year before, had gone on and on about the popcorn in Ecuador, saying it was so good he made it for dinner most nights.

Now I hate to admit it, but I am a bit of a popcorn snob. I have always been an 'Orville Redenbacher' girl, so I was anxious to find a pot and test the local stuff. After wading through the river of plastic we turned down an aisle and voila, there were forty different pots to choose from!

After we left Santa María, we found a heladería and bellied up to the ice-cream bar for a couple of cones. I got my favorite, menta (mint chocolate chip with chocolate chunks the size of hockey pucks), and Hugh got mango. The ice-cream was so good and rich we considered it lunch.

After we finished our helado, we stumbled upon a little boutique coffee and chocolate store. We were able to sample about a dozen different kinds of chocolate (you can never have too much chocolate, right?) made from different regions of the country. Our favorite was an 85% dark variety made in the Galapagos. While we were there we ordered Ecuadorian coffee, and YES! It was brewed right in front of our eyes. The smell was lovely.

Hugh and I had brought enough cash with us to last our first month in the country, but we realized we needed to make sure our card worked at the ATM, just in case. Plus, we had no clue what the fees were going to look like. We had heard conflicting accounts of how much it cost to access money and were anxious to find out for ourselves.

We located a Banco de Guayaquil ATM and found out our card did, indeed, work. Whew! We were charged $1.50 to make a withdrawal, which was fine, but we were limited to $300.00 per day. Considering our total cost for riding four buses that day was $1.50 for the both of us, we didn't think the withdrawal cap would be a problem.

We got back to the penthouse feeling pretty good about the day. We were more confident navigating the city, we had survived the Iña Quito market, and we figured out the ATM deal. Plus, we had been serenaded and found a popcorn pot and some really yummy chocolate.

The next quest for this southern girl was to find some grits!

Day Nineteen: The Age of Connectivity

Day nineteen was an intense study day for several reasons. First, we considered it our job to learn as much of the native language as we could. That's only fair, right? Second, Hugh's left knee had swollen to the size of a large grapefruit and my right foot was still smarting from a spill I had taken a couple of weeks before we left the states (Howard and Ammie, that was one hell of a send-off dinner!). So Hugh and I decided it would be a good day to study Spanish and ice our complaining body parts.

But after a morning of making a couple hundred or so Spanish vocabulary note cards, we were both getting a little stir crazy in the penthouse. We decided to get some fresh air and take our time climbing the hill to SuperMaxi.

The trip was worth it because we found Camembert cheese! OK, so it was 'Camembert-ish' and was made in Ibarra, but it wasn't bad. And once we slathered it on the fresh bread we got at our neighborhood panadería it was really quite tasty!

On the slow walk back down the hill, we started

thinking about what we missed from the states, besides our family and friends, of course. About all we could come up with was McCallan's Scotch, affordable wine, Arm and Hammer toothpaste, and the previously mentioned grits. We didn't even miss television. We were able to stream radio stations from the Carolinas on our computer, and had even been able to watch a few episodes of the BBC's *Sherlock* online whenever we needed a TV 'fix.' But other than that, we didn't miss much.

When we got back to the penthouse, we made new ice packs (for the parts that didn't particularly care for our walk that day) and I called my parents. They told me they were shooting for November to come visit us. Yay! Neither of my parents had ever traveled to South America, so this was going to be a huge deal for them. I couldn't wait.

After I finished talking with my parents, I called my good friend, Angela. I have known Angela since high school. In our younger days, she and I had a knack for getting OUT of trouble before anyone found out we were IN trouble to begin with.

Now, you have already become acquainted with Triplet, our international feline traveler and three-legged cat extraordinaire, but we had two other cats before we moved as well. Tiger and Lilly were litter-mates from a stray cat that thought my grandfather's outbuilding would be a great place to have her kittens. I fell in love with those two little fur-balls one day while visiting my grandfather and took them home to live with us.

When we decided to move to Ecuador I set out to find suitable homes for all three cats, but I really wanted to keep Tiger and Lilly together if I could. After all, they had only ever known a world in which the other existed.

If you plan on moving abroad, know that one of the most difficult things you will have to do is decide what to do with your pets. I know now I will never ever leave an animal behind again.

Angela originally said she would take Triplet, but the more I thought about it, the more I realized that wasn't such a great match. Angela is more of a 'dog' person and had three of them at the time. I didn't think that would be fair to our little handicapped kitty who had worked so hard to survive. Plus, I just had a feeling Triplet would be going to Ecuador with us.

About the time Hugh realized I wasn't going anywhere until I could find a suitable home for our feline siblings, Angela grew a bright pair of angel wings and said she would take Tiger *and* Lilly. I didn't worry so much about Angela's dogs with those two because they had been big buddies with our golden retriever, Bido, before he died. I will never be able to thank Angela enough for such a meaningful act of friendship.

So Triplet ended up being the queen of the penthouse

in Quito, and Tiger and Lilly had fun taunting the dogs at Angela's house in South Carolina!

Starting our adventure during an age of connectivity was a lifesaver for me. I don't know if we could have made the transition without the ability to tap into the internet to reach those we loved. How did people in the past travel such lengths and not suffer from severe homesickness? Of course, Skyping and hugging are not the same thing, but, for the moment, Skyping was better than nothing.

Day Twenty: My Parents are Adults

All (and I do mean ALL) of day twenty was spent trying to figure out possible flights to Ecuador for my parents. They were finally gung-ho to visit by the end of the year, which was great! We only had two problems.

1) My father wouldn't spend the night anywhere for a layover, and 2) my mother refused to fly in the dark. What? Now I have my own phobias, so I can't really judge theirs, but this sure did make things difficult, if not impossible.

Ecuador has two international airports, one in Quito, the other in Guayaquil. Everything would have been fine if we were still going to be living in Quito, but by the time my parents arrived we would already be in Cuenca. This meant my parents would have an extra leg from Quito (or Guayaquil) to Cuenca.

Now, at that time, the last international flight into Quito arrived around 8:00 PM every evening. Problem was, there were no late day or evening flights from Quito to Cuenca, which meant an overnight in Quito (not cool with my dad). Or they could spend about eighteen hours flying from Charlotte to New York to Guayaquil to Cuenca, but they would have to fly through the night (not cool with my mom). Either way we were at an impasse, and unfortunately, there weren't any other options.

About the time my head was about to explode I remembered my parents were adults. If they wanted to visit their daughter in South America they would find a way.

Days Twenty-one ~ Thirty

Day Twenty-one: City Noise

I'm sure you will not be surprised when I say, another day, another trip to SuperMaxi! We could take various routes to get there, and we often did to break up the monotony, but in reality, all the streets looked essentially the same no matter which way we went.

All residences were gated at the sidewalk. The only difference was whether the gate was solid or barred, spiky or booby trapped with broken glass or electricity (or both), and whether or not there was a small yard or a parking pad on the other side of the gate. If there was a yard, it was, at best, ten by fifteen feet. Some people forwent the yard and opted for flowering plants and shrubs, but if there was a solid gate, we had no clue whether or not they had a green area. Security is a very serious business in Ecuador.

If someone's house is robbed in Ecuador it is the homeowner's fault, not the robber's, because the homeowner didn't do a good enough job securing his or her property. If your pocket is picked, again, it is your fault because you should know to keep a better watch over your pockets.

This desire for security extends to their cars, which leads me to city noise. I'm not sure if this is a big city thing or an Ecuador thing, but I swear if we heard one car alarm a day we heard fifty. It was constant. Our friend, Max, likes to say the national bird of Ecuador is the car alarm. Of course, with so many alarms going off all the time no one pays any attention to them. Whoo-whoo-whoo-whoo-eeeeek-eeeeek-eeeeek-eeeeek-chakka-chakka-chakka-chakka-bip-bip-bip-bip all day long.

And while car alarms were some of the most annoying sounds in Quito, they weren't the only ones. Think blaring house alarms while residents are away for a long weekend and can't be reached to turn the dang thing off. Think party music from the house down the street until three in the morning. And do the squeaky raw milk trucks have to make their rounds before the sun comes up?

People in Ecuador are not shy about giving their horns a workout in traffic, either. If the car at the light doesn't move the exact second the light changes it sets off a chain reaction of angry honks from all directions.

Safety tip! If you are a pedestrian, well, all I can say is, drivers own the roads in Ecuador. It is *your* responsibility, Mr. Pedestrian, not to get run over. Seriously. NO ONE stops, or even yields, for pedestrians.

And then there is the incessant beeping of natural gas trucks seven days a week. Most Ecuadorian households use gas for stoves and showers (if they are lucky enough not to have a Frankenstein). But the good news is government subsidies ensure a forty pound tank of gas will only set you back about $2.50.

It took me two weeks to figure out what the deliberate and cyclic series of honks was circling around the neighborhood at all hours, like a vulture looking for roadkill. Some of the gas truck drivers had a gentle reminder of three honks every block, while more insistent drivers could deliver up to a dozen hostile honks every half block. I didn't know if the frequency of honks was driven more by personality or by quota, but either way, it contributed greatly to the noise fabric of the city.

And then there were the buses, which assaulted both ears and nose. But buses are an essential part of life in Ecuador, so we decided we better get used to them. And, like most things in life, the sooner you accept something the better off you are. We enjoyed riding the bus, or at any rate, didn't mind it that much, especially since it was a super cheap way to get from point A to point B.

Now all these things, the noise, the pollution, the personal accountability, are common in big cities, especially in South America. But it took this small-town southern girl a little time to get used to it!

Triplet had a great day twenty-one because she caught a fly, which is no small accomplishment for a three-legged cat. Of course, the flies are pretty slow at that altitude and Hugh happened to bat it on the ground for her, but she was proud of herself and enjoyed the impromptu kitty snack!

Day Twenty-two Part One: New Bus Adventures and Can We PLEASE Buy This Corkscrew?

We woke up to a bright, sunny view of the mountains, and even though the forecast called for a chance of rain, Hugh and I didn't count on it. It hadn't rained at all since we had moved to Quito, and the air was getting pretty dusty, a fact my contact lenses reminded me of several times daily.

I realized after breakfast that I had no idea what I weighed any more. I didn't even know what I looked like body-wise because we didn't have a full-length mirror, only a small one on the medicine cabinet in the bathroom.

I don't consider myself to be an extremely vain person, but I do try to keep fit, and being barely five feet tall any weight I gain can only go OUT. I had been in the habit of weighing daily in the states, partly out of curiosity, but also so that I could adjust my portion size during the day if need be to stay on track. I knew Hugh had lost some weight since we had been in Quito because I could see him. I wasn't worried about it because my clothes still fit, we walked all the time, and I was doing yoga every morning, so I knew I hadn't gained much, if any. I found it refreshing not to be so concerned about my weight anymore.

After studying Spanish and quick-soaking some dried beans for dinner that night, we decided to go to the Mercado Artesanal off the Avenida de las Amazonas. María had told us it was a great little market.

We had some interesting bus rides that morning on the way to town.

Two young guys with a big radio box and a pan flute followed us onto our first bus that day. The taller of the two (he was about my size) started the music and changed the tracks while the other fellow played the pan flute along with the recording, kind of like karaoke with a pan flute instead of a voice. The first song was, what I think of as a Simon and Garfunkel song, *El Condor Pasa*. This tune is actually based on a Peruvian Andean folk song and is now the second national anthem of Peru. The songs *Moon River* and *Greensleeves* were also in the man's repertoire. I think the men sold three CDs on our bus that day.

After they got off, a guy with a dozen cheap silver plated rings lining his fingers jumped on and started his spiel about what wonderful jewelry he had (of course, it was made in China). He darted up and down the aisle slipping rings on the fingers of uninterested men and women and was so loud and twitchy I don't think anyone bought anything from him that day.

Then a hefty, but bursting at the seams with personality, spiky-haired teenager got on the bus with a boom box and entertained us with South American hip-hop! He wasn't bad until he went into his falsetto voice that was, well, very odd and not particularly pleasant. I think he only made about fifty cents on that ride, but he was happy to fist bump everyone just the same.

The next stop brought us a thin greasy haired man selling meat pies. Now based on the amount of grease he had on his head I certainly wasn't going to support his pie business.

Before we went to the Artisans' Market, we revisited the mall where we bought our cheapy phones that day with María. The whole mall was built in a circle and spiraled round and round to the top. There were no stairs, just a continuous curved ramp. We strolled to the top that day, peeked in some windows, and noticed how the storefronts were narrow but then widened towards the back like pie wedges.

We were about three-quarters of the way up when we noticed a shop that had executive looking merchandise. You know, things for a vice-president's desk, like pen sets, glass chess boards, and stuff for an office bar. That's when it hit me. Maybe they had a corkscrew!

Sure enough, they had what we were looking for. A plain fold up corkscrew with a bottle opener on the other end. Yay! So we asked the very young salesperson (she was maybe 14) how much the corkscrew cost, and after she referred to a pricing guide she said it was $3.00. We thought that was reasonable, so Hugh started to pull out his money, but she abruptly said, "Espere!" Come to find out, she had the wrong list. So we waited about fifteen minutes while she looked for the *real* price.

What happened next was just plain bizarre. She took the corkscrew back and told us she couldn't sell it to us. If it wasn't on the list it wasn't for sale. We asked if she could, maybe, call someone and ask how much it was? I mean, come on, there were six corkscrews there on display. They had to be for sale! But, no. She wouldn't call anyone. Looked like Hugh was doomed to open our wine bottles with that stupid paring knife and his teeth.

Day Twenty-two Part Two: The Artisans' Market

We were anxious to get out of the mall after the corkscrew debacle, so we headed on over to the Artisans' Market. This covered market was arranged in tight rows, with the vendors' booths spilling merchandise out into the narrow aisles. The rows were so tight Hugh and I had to walk single file.

The market reminded me of a kaleidoscope with so many bright colors jumping out at us. Alpaca and cotton blankets were stacked row after row up to the ceiling, mannequins wore up to twenty straw hats on their bald heads, and rainbow colored beads and silver bracelets and rings shimmered in the filtered sunlight.

There were handmade leather shoes, painted canvas shoes, woven sandals, deep brown and green leather bound handmade notebooks, pan flutes and wooden drums, embroidered blouses, purple, green, and yellow geodes, brightly painted chess sets with Incan soldiers as the pawns. And then there was the constant sound of the vendors' voices trying to lure you, tempt you, guilt you into staying at their booth for only twenty seconds more. Oh, and ice cream! The market had lots and lots of ice cream.

Did I see anything I'd like to buy? Of course, I did. But since we would be (hopefully) moving in a few weeks, I decided to just have fun watching people interact. And, honestly, most of the people we saw that day were as 'colorful' as the merchandise.

After a while, we grabbed some gelato (mango and pistachio) and got back on the bus. We were expecting more bus entertainment, but instead, we had to find our entertainment by looking out the bus windows.

We saw old women selling cards and cards of lottery tickets, black skirted indigenous women pushing wheelbarrows full of naranjas and fresas (oranges and strawberries), and little boys selling phone chargers on the corner. Black-hatted men weaved in and out of traffic selling brooms, energy bars, and red cloths for drying cars. We saw small children clinging to their mothers' skirts, young mothers breastfeeding in the median with the cars and buses zooming by, and men with water bottles vying to clean car windshields.

Yes, it was a busy, crazy, and fun afternoon in downtown Quito!

Day Twenty-two Part Three: Stupid Black Beans

After we got home that afternoon, I took beans I had soaked that morning, rinsed them, and put them on the stove to cook. We planned to eat dinner a couple hours later, and in our previous life, that was not an unreasonable expectation.

Hugh checked the beans an hour later, and, with a quizzical look on his face, informed me that they were still *very* hard. I wasn't worried about it, so they continued to cook while we worked on other parts of dinner. An hour later, the beans were no better than pebbles.

What the heck was going on with the beans? We had no clue, so I did what you do these days when you can't figure something out. I googled it.

Come to find out, the high altitude in Quito is not a friend to dried beans. Not only do beans need to soak for a *very* long time, they apparently need to cook for several days. Not hours. DAYS. They weren't kidding about 'mañana' around there.

So we ate rice without the stupid black beans for dinner, and I went to bed wondering what other culinary surprises we might discover in the weeks and months ahead.

Day Twenty-three: A Lumpy Rainstorm

I got up extra early that morning to start those stupid beans again. I was determined that, one way or another, we would have black beans for dinner that night.

As we were getting ready for our daily SuperMaxi run, Hugh noticed some dark clouds gathering in the distance. We still had not had any rain since we had been in the country so we were hopeful that it might actually rain that afternoon. On the way out the door, I grabbed the cute little hot pink TOTES umbrella I used to keep in my car (when I had a car), you know, just in case.

The clouds got angrier as we hiked up the hill that morning. But with any luck, it would rain while we were in the grocery store and be done by the time we finished our shopping.

In the store, we had just made it to the produce section when all hell broke loose. The sound beating against the roof was deafening. Even the Ecuadorians in the store looked startled by the intensity of the storm.

With all that rain we knew we wouldn't be going

anywhere anytime soon, so we piddled around, and looked at, well, just about everything in the store. Twice. Finally, the sound of the storm eased, so we paid for our groceries and set out.

As soon as we stepped outside I knew something was off. The ground was lumpy. The sound we heard in the store wasn't rain, it was hail. Two inches of marble sized hail covered the parking lot. It was then I realized how cold it had become.

It was still raining some at this point, and unfortunately, I had forgotten how 'little' my cute little hot pink umbrella was. It covered half of me, and about a quarter of Hugh. That was a loooong walk home. Of course, the rain stopped at the exact moment we turned onto our street.

So, after cooking an additional thirteen hours that day the beans were still crunchy. But Hugh and I ate those black beans for dinner anyway. Stupid beans.

I was supposed to Skype my good friends, Stephanie and Linda, after dinner that day, but when I opened up my laptop I discovered there was no wifi connection. Storm related? Maybe. Guess we would find out mañana.

Day Twenty-four: Graffiti, Mountain Living, and a Missing Sock

We still had no wifi the next morning, so we decided to go to an internet café so my mother wouldn't freak out when she didn't hear from me (I sent her a little note every day so she wouldn't worry). Internet cafés are really popular in Ecuador. Most Ecuadorians don't have computers, but at forty cents an hour at an internet café, most everyone can have access to the rest of the world without having to invest in a machine.

We got caught up on our correspondences then took our laundry to Valeria, our new friend at the lavandería. I tried to sneak a little of my Spanish in, but, of course, all she wanted to do was speak English.

Since a lot of our language studying was done online, and we had no online, we thought we would catch a bus we had never ridden and just go wherever it went. We started out on our regular blue bus to the Avenida de las Amazonas where we would have a large number of lines to choose from.

The more we rode the bus, the more we were able to study our environment. First that day, we noticed everything looked a lot brighter and cleaner after the storm. But then, for some reason, what jumped out at me was the copious amount of graffiti in the capital city.

The graffiti ranged from uncreative and amateurish to sensitive and beautiful. Mixed in with the predictable and boring professions of eternal love (Carlita, te amo simpre), aimless squiggles, and so-and-so is numero uno!, there was some amazing art.

Some of the graffiti I noticed that morning depicted elaborate flower bouquets, cartoon characters from outer space, detailed sea life scenes, punk skulls, blue dragons, a floating girl with a green lollipop between her toes, angry fists, and soccer scenes. There were portraits of indigenous people and political quotes. Robots and smokey eyes searching from the dark, little boys reading books while riding balloons. Party announcements were painted for all to see. Love and sex scenes (some quite graphic) were interspersed between the family scenes and bible quotes. A stray dog took a leak on a wall where a toothy whale was eating an octopus.

We expected to find the advertisements at the bus stops vandalized as well, but the graffiti artists left those alone, although light posts were not immune to their poetic expression. I found it funny that, for the most part, these artists only managed to cover the bottom half of the walls. Guess ladders aren't as easy to carry around as spray paint.

Another thing we had noticed on our bus rides was the many different ways people dressed. Indigenous women have a dress code (for lack of a better word) depending on which 'tribe' they belong to. Some women wear long, straight black skirts with turquoise shirts, red shawls, and a black felt hat. Others wear knee-length fuzzy green pleated skirts (which make a cool swishing sound when they walk) with elaborately embroidered white blouses. Seeing little girls dressed like this was one of the cutest things I'd ever seen.

Most women in Ecuador keep their hair very long. The indigenous women either wear two braids, one near each ear, or a single braid down their back, which, along with their dress, helps you identify their tribe. I was often reminded of my great-grandmother, who was part Cherokee, when I saw those women around town.

The rest of the female population seemed to follow only one fashion rule, which is wear your clothes as tight as possible and show your 'assets.' It doesn't matter the body type, age, or weight of the person, TIGHT is RIGHT! And I have NO idea how these women managed to keep both legs in working order as they traversed up and down the uneven cobblestone streets and jumped in and out of buses in their stiletto heels (sometimes while breastfeeding!).

Ecuadorian men also wear their clothes on the tight side, and, unfortunately, many of the teenagers below the equator have subscribed to the tired style of having your pants hang off your ass so that you have to waddle to keep them from falling down. They looked like a bunch of drunk ducks to me.

Since we didn't have anything else to do that afternoon, we decided to ride the bus all the way to the end of the line to see how far it went. It went farther up the hill than we thought, through two whole other towns.

As we climbed higher up the hill we noticed the houses got smaller and farther apart, and there were more dogs running around. Ecuador doesn't really have any leash laws, so dogs just roam free.

We remembered something Sarah had told us about who lives in town vs. who lives up the mountain. In the states, most people that belong to the higher income bracket want a house OUT of town, and if you can afford a mountain house, you want one, in part, for the awesome view. People that are on the lower end of the economic ladder seem to live IN town with small yards in cramped neighborhoods with no view.

In Ecuador, however, the 'higher-ups' want to live in town and don't care about a view, and the 'lower-downs' live in depressed housing away from town but have a drop-dead gorgeous view of the surrounding mountains.

That's exactly what we observed as we came back down the mountain. The view was incredibly beautiful, but the houses were little cinderblock shacks with trash-filled yards and dirt floors.

We got back to our neck of the woods right before dark and remembered we had laundry to pick up. While putting up our clothes, I found a sock dancing solo. Now I didn't take that many socks with me, so I needed to find that sock. Hugh assured me my MIA sock was hiding out at the laundry, and we could check mañana.

That was fine with me. After sitting on a bumpy bus most of the day, my bum was ready for bed.

Day Twenty-five: Independence Day

Happy Independence Day! On this day, August 10, 1809, rebels in the city of Quito fought against French rule by displacing the representatives of Joseph Bonaparte, Napoleon's older brother. Although true independence for the entire country wouldn't come right away, this was the beginning for, not only Quito but the entire country, so this day is celebrated in Ecuador from the coast to the Amazon.

After dropping my 'independent' sock off at the laundry to hopefully find its mate, we decided to commemorate the occasion by heading back to Old Town and having lunch in a Cantonese restaurant. The portions were huge, the food was muy rico, and we were entertained by the Ecuadorian equivalent of WWF Smackdown on a small television that hung from the restaurant ceiling.

Not sure why, but that Saturday we saw about a dozen jugglers in the streets. When I say in the streets, I mean IN the streets. Some had bright orange pins, others had little yellow fluorescent balls or coconuts, one guy was juggling machetes, and a very young girl was twirling brightly colored flags. Unfortunately, we missed the fire show; that guy was already packing up.

Hugh and I had been wanting to go back to the Basílica del Voto National so that we could spend more time looking around inside, so that's where we headed after lunch. We walked past the woman on the steps selling rosaries and candles, paid our dollar to enter, then spent the next forty-five minutes walking around that big, beautiful homage to God and saints and virgins.

We arrived as a service was beginning, but I guess the locals are used to tourists because they didn't even acknowledge the strangers wandering around. The priest was speaking into a microphone, and there was a painting of Jesus above the pulpit that was illuminated by a blinking red light. I thought that was strange, but we would go on to visit other churches in Ecuador, and some of them even had bright neon florescent signs above classical religious paintings.

Bright and elaborate stained glass windows offered bible scenes high up the walls and on the ceiling, and every marble column presented an oil painting depicting a specific suffering of Christ. There were mausoleums and doll statues of local virgins with flowers, burning candles, and collection cups in the recesses.

The thing that struck me most that afternoon were two dark, colossal wood doors at one end of the sanctuary.

The sun was right behind those doors and shot bright sun rays like lasers through the wood cracks and glass work, which made the marble floor in front of the doors sparkle and shimmer like sunshine on a pond.

After we left the Basílica, we headed back to 'Luz de Vida,' our favorite little coffee shop in Old Town. The owner, Oscar, enthusiastically greeted us, and Hugh took a picture of Oscar and me to post on Facebook. Very nice man, and great coffee. We hoped Cuenca would have a little coffee shop that made us feel so welcome.

The bus trip home was a quiet one. We had expected to see, well, I'm not sure what we expected to see on that Independence Day in Quito. Other than the jugglers and a greater number of Ecuadorian flags, everything else seemed to be the same as it was during the week. Visa Nora later told us the president of Ecuador had decided the 'official' government sanctioned celebrations should be observed in May when the final battle for independence took place. We would have to wait until the following year to see the 'real' independence celebrations.

We stopped by the laundry on the way back to the penthouse to see if my sock had been reunited with its mate. Valeria's padre shrugged and said, "Maybe mañana."

We had only been home about thirty minutes when very loud, aggressive, bass-heavy music began shaking the windows. This was an edgy, rock-punk-reggae sound that continued until after midnight. Now I am a musician and appreciate many different types of music, but this 'music' was difficult to swallow, especially for six hours.

I wondered if Ecuadorians always celebrated their day of independence with loud reggae music. But, hey, who am I to judge?

Day Twenty-six: Head Bangin'

Day twenty-six began as a lovely, lazy, quiet Sunday morning. After yoga, breakfast, and a few online chess games and some sudoku, we ventured out to, you guessed it, SuperMaxi, where we discovered we need to be anywhere other than the grocery store at noon on a Sunday. Busy, busy busy!

On the way home, we stopped at a little pink painted cinderblock heladería a block from the grocery store. We piled our groceries bags in the corner and looked at all the different kinds of ice cream they were serving that day. The young guy behind the counter kept offering us samples, and I swear, after all the free ice cream we were almost too full to order anything else. But we didn't want to be rude, so I tried the mora (blackberry) and Hugh got pistachio.

One thing I was still trying to get used to in Ecuador was the pervasive presence of armed guards everywhere, and I do mean *everywhere*. Grocery stores, pharmacies, butcher shops, malls, parks, even cute little pink ice cream shops. These men (rarely women) were armed with automatic weapons and serious kick-ass boots. They were protected by bulletproof vests and make-my-day-punk attitudes.

Ecuadorians don't have the second amendment, so the general public is not allowed to possess guns. And while it was a little disconcerting to see this serious display of force to begin with, I can honestly say we felt pretty safe walking around the streets of Quito.

On the way home after our ice cream lunch, we ran into María. She had just gotten back from visiting her brother, who lived about an hour out of town in el campo (the countryside). She asked us to stop by her apartment when we finished our errands because her brother had sent a big box of fruit home with her to give to us. María had told him about her new friends from the states, and this was his way of welcoming us to his country.

María met us at her gate with a box so heavy with fruit Hugh and I struggled to get it up the stairs to the penthouse. Julio, María's brother, owned several fruit and vegetable stands and sent us bananas, kiwi, papaya, oranges, tangerines, pears, tree tomatoes, and a couple other native fruits we weren't yet familiar with. What a yummy and thoughtful welcome from a stranger!

The rest of the afternoon was low key and relaxing, until about 5:00 when the 'music' started up again. This time, however, there was no reggae element, just loud thumpin' bass with booming drums and screaming guitars.

Now I have been known to sing along with Ozzy Osbourne on the radio, but this 'music' was like the first few bars of Iron Man on a perpetual steroid loop. This guttural, gravelly, fingernails-on-chalkboard assault went on and on for hours with our windows and doors shaking the whole time.

After about six hours of this nonsense, I became a tad bit grumpy and vowed if this continued into the next day we would have to move, I didn't care where, just away from the madness. Poor Triplet couldn't cover her ears, no matter how hard she tried. It was a rough evening.

Turned out, the weekend 'music festival' was part of the city's independence celebration. The previous year it had been held at Parque Carolina off the Avenida de las Amazonas, but for some strange reason, the people who lived around there suggested the venue be changed to the new park at the old airport. Considerate, huh?

Can't say I blame them. But I suspected, if our neighbors felt as we did, they would probably have to relocate the festival again the following year. I just hoped they wouldn't end up in Cuenca.

Day Twenty-seven: A Multi-Pronged Approach

To everyone who ever told me learning Spanish would be easy I have only one thing to say. You obviously don't know what you're talking about!

Of course, I'm kidding, but learning Spanish was so much more difficult than I imagined. For example, Spanish has this thing called the personal 'a,' which is a pointless use of a perfectly good letter in a weird place. And the word 'agua' is feminine, right? So why is it incorrect to say 'la agua?' Did you know that double and even *triple* negatives are allowed in Spanish? I had a lot to learn.

But I wasn't going to let Spanish get the better of me, oh no. I decided to pull out all the stops and employ a multi-pronged approach.

I studied with the owl at duolingo. I read the books *Madrigal's Magic Key to Spanish* by Margarita Madrigal (whimsically illustrated by none other than Andy Warhol) and *Easy Spanish Step-By-Step* by Barbara Bregstein. I made over 300 note cards. I counted my breaths in Spanish when I practiced yoga. I eavesdropped on conversations while riding the bus. I forced myself to read grocery labels in Spanish and looked up every word I didn't know. We kept a Spanish newspaper in the bathroom. I pored over the fashion ads in the magazine Siempre Mujer. I called Triplet my 'gatita negra' and even attempted to teach her the correct way to meow in Spanish...miau, miau!

Truth is, I enjoyed it. I am a geek when it comes to learning new things and I was having a blast with the Spanish language, even though it wasn't easy. It's true that Spanish is similar to English in a lot of ways, but the longer I studied the more different the languages became.

But, since I wasn't working a 'real' job, I considered it my duty to make as much progress in the communications department as I could. After all, isn't that what most people expect of immigrants in other countries?

I can't describe the joy I felt the first time I was able to tell the indigenous woman at the corner mercado what I wanted in Spanish and she understood me! That was chevere (cool)!

Even though the previous few days had been difficult, again, it wasn't really anything we hadn't expected or couldn't deal with (except the head bangin' music...that was horrible.) The Ecuadorian people were warm and delightful, and we were still happy with our decision to move to

Ecuador.

Yes, we were settling into our new norm of studying Spanish and waiting for word from Visa Nora about our residency status. Luckily, we wouldn't have to wait too much longer.

Day Twenty-eight: The Roof Saga

We spent most of the day looking for a vegetarian restaurant we passed by in downtown Quito several days prior. We knew we didn't dream the place up because we both physically entered the restaurant and looked at a menu. Somehow, though, the restaurant had vanished.

We settled on a cute little Mexican/Italian place that had a few vegetarian options. I had a veggie burrito, and Hugh had meat lasagne. We then had coffee (the dreaded instant), watched people walk by, and wondered where the other restaurant could have gone. We would later learn that businesses in Ecuador are a bit fickle, and often move or disappear with no warning.

On the bus home, we were serenaded by two rappers for Jesus, complete with baggy pants and boom box. It must have been holy-roller day because later on we were entertained by the Ecuadorian version of a fire and brimstone preacher. I couldn't understand exactly what he was saying, but he was really angry about something and was pretty sure we were all going to hell.

Back at the penthouse, we tuned in to the 'roof saga.' For the last couple of weeks, we had been watching a couple of men fix a roof one street over from the penthouse.

The roofs in Quito are overwhelmingly flat. They basically serve as a patio area, and this is where people wash and hang their laundry and let their kids play. People even keep their dogs up there since they don't have yards. These roofs are cement with drains routed down to the street to siphon water after it rains.

Our tiny apartment, um, penthouse, was basically an extra room that someone had, at some point, stuck on top of the roof. And even though it hadn't been ideal, I have to admit the 'penthouse view' had been astounding. We had a full view of the volcano Cotopaxi and could see fireworks every night in the many small towns that surrounded the city (Ecuadorians love fireworks). We also had front row seats for the 'roof saga.'

One morning we woke up to a very consistent tap, BANG, tap. When we looked out the big picture window by our bed we saw two men sitting on the roof a couple of buildings over. They both had chisels and five-pound hammers and proceeded to chip away at that roof for over a week. Tap, tap, BANG, tap, chip, tap, tap, BANG, chip, chip, BANG.

Eventually, another man appeared and hauled all the broken concrete away. Then the first two guys hauled fifty-pound bags of mortar to the roof on their shoulders. I wouldn't have trusted the handmade rickety wooden ladder they used, but they didn't seem to mind.

The following two days involved one guy mixing and spreading the new cement on the roof while two other men passed bucket after bucket of water up to him via that wobbly ladder. Thankfully, on our twenty-eighth day in the country, the men spread plastic over the entire roof which meant the job was finished.

I thought there must be a machine that could have knocked that job out in a day, but Hugh said he figured manual labor was so cheap it was probably a cost effective way to get something done, especially since Ecuadorians don't mind how long things take to finish, you know, with mañana and all. And of course, everyone had a friend or a cousin who needed work. So I guess it was a win-win for all involved.

It was fun watching the progress of the men every day, but I'll admit we were happy when all that tapping and banging stopped. Triplet was, too!

Day Twenty-nine: Meds and Morocho Fino

I woke with a small headache and realized we were getting low on the ibuprofen we brought with us from the states. So we stopped by the pharmacy near SuperMaxi with the intention of picking up some pain relievers.

Now, theoretically, you can get about anything you want at a farmacia in Ecuador without a prescription. All you have to do is tell the pharmacist what's going on and they will give you something. You can even ask for what you want specifically, like HRT, valium, prozac, even 'little blue pills.'

However, the pharmacist told us that morning that we would need a prescription for any anti-inflammatory drug. What? I could buy viagra but I couldn't buy ibuprofen?

We finally found out that once a year during flu season the government tries to prevent people from self-medicating by restricting non-steroidal pain killers. After all, if a person feels better they might get on a bus and infect sixty other people. I kind of understood, but I still had a headache.

So we went to another farmacia four doors down from

the first one and the pharmacist gave me what I asked for right away. So we learned if you don't get what you want in one place, don't fret, just go somewhere else. And it pretty much worked like that the whole time we were in Ecuador.

After we scored at the second pharmacy, we decided to see if my errant sock had reappeared at the laundry. Valeria's father smiled and said, "Sólo un calcetín." Only one sock.

On an interesting note, the word 'calcetín' is a bit outdated in Ecuador. Valeria called them 'medias.' But, whatever they were called, one of them was still lost.

What else could I say but, "No hay problema." He responded with, "See you Friday."

But, on a good note, we found grits! Yay! Of course, they aren't called grits in Ecuador, they are called morocho fino. They were hiding out on the rice aisle, of all places. Desafortunadamente (that was my new favorite eight-syllable Spanish word), we had already eaten breakfast that morning, but I could finally look forward to eating grits!

And, on an even better note, María called to tell us that her brother, Julio (the one who gave us all the fruit), was willing to move us to Cuenca in his vegetable truck! We still had a little time but realized we needed to go ahead and get our moving plans finalized soon, which made us further realize there were still things we wanted to do and places we wanted to visit before we left that part of the country.

Day Thirty: Felicidades!

Finally. Grits for breakfast! And they were every bit as good as we remembered. Now, I thought, if I could only learn to make decent pancakes at that altitude we would be set in the desayuno department.

After breakfast, Hugh went to leave a note for Patricio. Our internet had been out for several days (again), and we were getting tired of having to go to the internet café several times a day.

Patricio knocked on our door about an hour later and confirmed there had been a problem before, but it had since been fixed. However, in the process of fixing the original problem, Nora Landlady had gotten a new username and password for her wifi but had neglected to tell us about it. We had been using the old username and password! So, after several attempts, we had our connection back and Patricio went on his way.

We got our internet back at just the right moment, too, because we had news for our friends and family back home. Our residency visas had been approved! Felicidades to us! I don't know how to convey what a relief it was to know that part of our journey was over. We didn't have to apply (and pay) for an extension to our tourist visas because we were perfectly legitimate Ecuadorian residents. Yay!

On top of our good news, María called that afternoon to ask if we would come over to her house for breakfast the following morning. Being invited into an Ecuadorian home is a BIG deal. You do not get invited into an Ecuadorian's home unless you are considered family. Of course, we told María we would be delighted! We had had our ups and downs living in Quito, but meeting María was definitely the best of the ups.

And if that wasn't good enough, Hugh and I both realized that morning we had made it up the four flights of stairs to the penthouse without feeling like we were about to go into cardiac arrest. We had finally learned to breathe at 9,000 feet!

Thirty days in Quito. Wow. What a month!

Epilogue

We had another two weeks in Quito before we headed south to Cuenca. We spent most of that time visiting museums, parks, and cathedrals in Old Town. We did make it to Mitad del Mundo with María and took an overnight trip to Otavalo where we had a crazy fun time at one of the largest open-air markets in South America.

We also spent several days in Mindo, a cute little hippie town that had some of the best pizza I'd ever tasted. We hiked, rode a crazy zipline (I even did 'tricks,' believe it or not!), visited a butterfly farm, took a chocolate tour, and had a blast bird-watching at our hostel. We took Triplet with us and she had a grand time chasing after all the little bugs that thrived in the lower altitude.

Nora Landlady was sweet the day we left Quito and gave us each parting gifts. And Patricio and his cute little family were there to bid us farewell the day we loaded ourselves, our belongings, and Triplet into Julio's vegetable truck to move to Cuenca.

After Visa Nora took us to pick up our residency

papers, we never heard from her again. About a year later we found out that her husband had been arrested for human trafficking and was serving time in a federal prison in Florida. No wonder we didn't hear from her.

We kept in touch with our dear friend María after we moved to Cuenca, and I spoke with her often. One day she called to tell me she had cancer. I was heartbroken when she died two years later.

Hugh and I had many adventures after we moved to Cuenca, and we made many wonderful friends, both Ecuadorians and expats, from all over the world. But that's another story.

After three years in Ecuador, we felt the call of home. We returned to South Carolina in the fall of 2016 with Triplet and her Ecuadorian baby brother, Puck, a gray tabby Hugh rescued in Cuenca. I'd like to say she approves of the addition to the family, but she pretty much hates his guts.

I believe I am a better person because of our time spent in Ecuador. I know I am a more rounded person, a more knowledgeable person, a more patient person. And I owe it all to a free spirit named Hugh. Thank you, darling, for the experience of a lifetime.

One Last Thing...

Thank you for reading about my adventures in Ecuador! If you enjoyed *Thirty Days In Quito: Two Gringos and a Three-Legged Cat Move to Ecuador,* I'd be grateful if you would post a short review on Amazon. Your support and comments really make a difference, especially to indie authors!

I would also appreciate good old-fashioned 'word of mouth' to your friends, colleagues, and anyone else you think might enjoy reading about other cultures and moving abroad.

Happy traveling!

Wait! Turn the page for a bonus...

A Bonus!

Did you know I also write fiction? As a thank you for reading my book, *Thirty Days in Quito: Two Gringos and a Three-Legged Cat Move to Ecuador*, I'd like to give you a free humorous short story I wrote that explores some of the problems that expats face while living in other countries.

If you enjoy my story, *Muffin Top*, you can get another FREE short story by joining my other subscribers at www.kkrisloomis.com. I send out two (and only two!) updates a month about what's going on in my writing world, and you will also have opportunities to receive free advance copies of future projects and help me choose titles and covers for my next books!

My collection of short stories, *The Monster In the Closet and Other Stories*, is available in both Kindle and paperback at Amazon.com!

Thanks again for your support!

Muffin Top

"Hey, Sylvia! You about done in there? It's almost time to meet the Petersons," Frank yells over his shoulder as he adjusts his tie in the dresser mirror.

A weak voice responds, "I'm not feeling well, Frank."

Frank rips his tie off and unbuttons the top button of his shirt. "What's wrong?" he asks.

"My tummy feels a little…strange," Sylvia answers from behind the closed door.

"Did you eat chochos from that street vendor again?" Frank asks his wife. "You know you shouldn't eat anything off the street."

"No, Frank, I didn't eat chochos from that street vendor again."

Frank crosses to the bathroom door and shouts, "Then what's wrong? We've eaten the same things and I feel just fine. And all that walking today has made me hungry as a horse." He pauses, then asks, "Hey, Sylvia, do they eat horse in Ecuador?"

"I don't think so, Frank. And I don't know what's wrong. I have some gurgling."

"Gurgling, huh? Probably just gas. You know the high altitude makes us gringos fart more." Frank walks back to the mirror and attempts to tie his tie again.

"This is more than gas, Frank." She pauses. "I don't think I should go."

"Don't be ridiculous! We've been looking forward to this evening with the Petersons for weeks!" Frank fumbles with the tie then decides he doesn't need one. He is, after all, retired. "Maybe a scotch would help. Huh, Sylvia? You want a scotch?"

Sylvia sighs. "No, Frank, I do not want a scotch."

Frank sits on the bed and puts his socks and shoes on. "Well, what can I do? We're supposed to meet Carol and John in thirty minutes. We've been looking forward to this special traditional dinner ever since we moved to South America. Hey, what about a Tums? I think there are still some Tums in the kitchen. I'll get you a Tums."

"I don't think Tums will help, Frank."

He walks to the bathroom door again. "What, Sylvia? Think you might have the worms?"

"Parasites. They're called PARASITES, Frank."

"Parasites, worms, what's the difference? You got some creepy crawlies goin' to town in your gut, that's what you got."

"I'll be fine, Frank. You go on without me."

Frank has an idea. "I know, Sylvia! Maybe that doctor fella down the hall is home. I'll go check."

Sylvia yells, "NO, Frank! I'm sure I'll be alright. I probably just need some rest. I'll be fine. I promise! I don't need a doctor!"

"Don't be ridiculous, Sylvia," Frank says to the door. "You remember that Yancy fella, we met him at Joe's? He got so dehydrated from his worms he ended up in the hospital. You know that can't be fun. So you just hang on and I'll go see if that Crespo fella's home."

Frank walks to the bedroom door as Sylvia shouts, "But, Frank! He doesn't speak English!"

"So? He's a doctor, isn't he? He had to take the hypocritical oath, didn't he?"

"HypoCRATic, Frank," she corrects for the umpteenth time.

"Yeah, whatever." Frank sees something on the dresser. "Besides, we have the translator on the iPad."

Frank steps out of the bedroom.

Sylvia yells, "But what if he's not at home?"

"Won't know until I knock!" Frank says as he slams the apartment door.

"Frank? FRANK!" Sylvia paces in the bathroom. "Oh, crap. I don't need a stinking' doctor, Frank! Oh, this isn't good. FRANK!!!"

She gives up and sits on the closed toilet lid.

Several minutes later Frank returns accompanied by a short Ecuadorian man dressed in jeans and a yellow soccer jersey. Sylvia hears them in the bedroom and puts her ear up to the door.

"Thanks for comin', Doc. I know it's the weekend and all, but I figure it's best to nip this worm thing in the bud, agreed?" Frank asks the good doctor.

The doctor looks around the bedroom. "¿Donde está la paciente?"

Frank stares at the doctor.

"La paciente, ¿donde está?"

"He wants to know where the patient is, Frank," Sylvia yells through the door.

"Oh." Frank motions to the door with a hitchhiker's thumb. "She's in the john."

The doctor nods. "¿Por cuanto tiempo ha estado enferma?"

Frank stares at the doctor again.

The doctor slowly repeats his question, "POR CUANTO TIEMPO HA ESTADO ENFERMA?"

"Wait!" Frank grabs the iPad off the dresser and holds it up to the doctor's face. "Say it again, Doc."

The doctor looks at the screen, then repeats the question a third time, "¿Por cuanto tiempo ha estado enferma?"

"He said how long have I been sick, Frank," Sylvia says from the bathroom.

Frank ignores her and reads off the iPad screen. "He wants to know how long you've been sick!"

Sylvia shakes her head. "Tell him I'm fine! I just need rest. Tell him to go home."

The doctor taps Frank on the shoulder. "El excremento…"

Frank shoves the iPad back in front of the doctor's nose.

"¿El excremento es marrón o verde?"

Frank crosses to the bathroom door and reads off the iPad, "He wants to know if your poo is brown or green!"

"¿Líquido o sólido?"

"Liquid or solid?"

"FRANK! This is ridiculous!" Sylvia can't believe this is happening.

"Now, Sylvia," Frank explains calmly to his wife behind the bathroom door, "these are simply medical questions. What should I tell him?"

Sylvia exhales through clenched teeth. "Tell him I have a little stomach upset, no big deal. I promise I'll be fine. Now just go ahead and meet the Petersons without me."

Frank gestures to the doctor to wait just a minute then turns back to the closed door. "Now, Sylvia. You know we promised each other we would do everything together once we retired and moved abroad. I *can't* go without you. Besides, I wouldn't want you to miss the feast!"

The doctor pulls a small plastic cup out of his bag and hands it to Frank. "Necesito una muestra."

"Uh, Sylvia," Frank says as he knocks on the door. "I think he needs a sample."

"A what!?"

"A stool sample. You're gonna have to open up."

Sylvia's stomach knots up for real. "Uh, wait! No. It's a mess in here. I'd be too embarrassed. You can't come in!"

"Now, Sylvia," Frank says as if speaking to a child. "How many times have you seen me endure the after effects of my chili cook-offs? We all gotta poo, and, well, sometimes it just ain't pretty. Now open up."

She yells in a last ditch effort to keep the men out of the bathroom, "But…but…it smells!"

"Whose shit doesn't?" Frank bangs on the door.

"SYLVIA!"

No response.

Frank looks at the doctor and motions to the door, "You try, Doc."

The doctor gently knocks and says in a sweet voice, "¿Señora? Necesito verla ahora. Necesito una muestra, por favor."

"NO!" Sylvia yells, then remembers her manners. "Gracias, I'm sure."

"No puedo ayudarla si no la puedo ver. La muestra es muy importante!"

"No."

The doctor looks at Frank and shrugs his shoulders.

"Women, go figure, right?" Frank says.

The doctor thinks he might understand. "Señora, ¿está en la menopausia?"

Sylvia flings the door open and says sternly, "Thank you, Doctor, but you can go home now."

"Sylvia, what's gotten into you?" Frank asks.

"Frank, please, just go without me," Sylvia begs her husband.

"But, Sylvia, we have been looking forward to this special cuy dinner for a long time…"

"NO, Frank. YOU have been looking forward to the

cuy dinner. Truth is…I do not want to eat cuy!" She falls face down on the bed and begins to cry.

Frank kneels down by the bed. "Why not? We've eaten lots of exotic dishes on our travels. You loved that fried tarantula in Cambodia, remember? And how 'bout those wasp crackers in Japan? Those were really tasty…"

"But I never had spiders or wasps as pets," she says through the sniffles. "I just can't eat a cousin of my precious Muffin Top!"

Frank is confused. "Who's Muffin Top?"

Sylvia sits up on the edge of the bed and fights back the tears as she explains, "Muffin Top was a sweet little guinea pig I had when I was a little girl. He was so cute (sniff sniff), and fuzzy (sniff), and he loved it when I gave him a b-b-belly rub!"

Frank takes his wife's hand and asks, "Why didn't you tell me this earlier?"

"I didn't want to d-d-disappoint you, Frank (sniff). I want you to enjoy retirement, and you get so much pleasure from eating weird things (sniff sniff). But I can't stop thinking about some little indigenous woman skinning M-M-Muffin Top and impaling him on one of those st-st-sticks!" Sylvia boo-hoos.

"Maybe you could just order a salad," Frank suggests.

"What, and watch YOU eat Muffin Top!?"

"OK, OK....it was just an idea. Calm down. Maybe we don't have to do everything together, after all." Frank reaches into his pocket for a handkerchief and hands it to Sylvia. She blows her nose and gives the hankie back to Frank.

The doctor has no idea what is going on but tries one more time. "Perdón, Señora, ¿la muestra?"

"Um, Doc, I don't think we need you anymore," Frank replies as he gets another handkerchief from the dresser.

The doctor shakes his head, so Frank speaks into the iPad and shows it to the doctor. The doctor nods then holds out his hand.

"Oh yeah, you want money," Frank says as he rummages through his pockets. He finally pulls out a hundred and holds it out for the doctor. "Here, Doc, all I got is this Franklin. You got change?"

The doctor shakes his head.

"Sylvia, you got change?" Frank asks his wife.

"No, Frank. The cab driver took all my change this morning."

"Hmmm." Frank has an idea.

"Hey, Doc. You like cuy?"

"¿Cuy? Sí, sabe muy bien!"

"Well, Doc, since my bride is, um, against eating her pet guinea pig from fifty years ago, how about you let me treat you to a nice cuy dinner?"

The doctor smiles and says, "OK!"

Frank turns to his wife. "I won't be late, Sylvia. You gonna be alright?"

Sylvia smiles at her husband. "I'll be fine, Frank. Now go enjoy your dinner."

Frank kisses Sylvia on the forehead then he and the doctor leave for their cuy dinner.

Sylvia takes a deep breath and looks around the room. She picks up her phone off the nightstand and dials.

"Fabianos? I'd like to order a pizza, please."

Get another **FREE** short story at www.kkrisloomis.com!

About the Author

Along with pursuing her lifelong dream of becoming a writer, K. Kris Loomis is a determined chess player, an origami enthusiast, a classically trained pianist, and a playwright. She helps busy people find time for yoga and meditation in her nonfiction writing and provides bite-sized short stories for time-crunched fiction lovers in her fiction writing.

Kris lives in South Carolina with her husband and two cats (including Triplet, feline extraordinaire and star of *Thirty Days In Quito: Two Gringos and a Three-Legged Cat Move to Ecuador!*).

You can see of Kris' current book selection at her Amazon author page at www.amazon.com/author/kkrisloomis.

Visit Kris' website at www.kkrisloomis.com and receive a FREE short story! And you can find her on Facebook, Twitter, and Pinterest @kkrisloomis.